Yourself

Understanding and Interpreting Accounts

Roger Mason

www.inaweek.co.uk

IN A WEEK

Hodder Education

338 Euston Road, London NW1 3BH

Hodder Education is an Hachette UK company

First published in UK 2013 by Hodder Education

This edition published 2013

British Library Cataloguing in Publication Data: a catalogue record for this title is available from the British Library.

10 9 8 7 6 5 4 3 2 1

Hachette UK's policy is to use papers that are natural, renewable and recyclable products and made from wood grown in sustainable forests. The logging and manufacturing processes are expected to conform to the environmental regulations of the country of origin.

www.hoddereducation.co.uk

Typeset by Cenveo® Publisher Services.

Printed in Great Britain by CPI Group (UK) Ltd, Croydon, CR0 4YY.

Contents

Introduction

There has never been a time when managers, and indeed people in general, were more exposed to a multitude of financial statements than they are today. To take just one example, millions of people are investors, perhaps indirectly, and are sent accounts and financial information relating to the companies in which they invest. Even non-financial managers are often involved in budgeting and regular financial reporting. They are expected to understand the accounts put in front of them and to contribute to the analysis and interpretation of the figures.

It is important that managers understand the principles of analysing and interpreting accounts. They will then be able to deal with such questions as:

● Is our customer in trouble? Are we going to be paid?
● Profits are down – why exactly?
● Just what is gearing? And does it matter?

This book is written for managers wishing to answer these questions. By setting aside a little time each day for a week, you will greatly increase your understanding of accounts and how to interpret them.

This book has been written with reference to the law of the United Kingdom, and with reference to UK accounting standards and international accounting standards. Laws vary from country to country. Most but not all of the world uses international accounting standards. This book should be useful to all readers, but these differences should be kept in mind.

It will be a great help if you get hold of a set of accounts and examine them as explained in this book. It is likely to be more meaningful if the accounts are for a company that you know well, such as your employer. It is not difficult to obtain accounts and on Monday it is explained how this can be done.

The book contains 70 end-of-chapter questions, each with four possible answers. The correct answers are given at the end of the book. I do hope that you attempt them. If you get 60 correct, that is a good score – anything higher is exceptional.

I have enjoyed writing this book and I hope that you enjoy reading it, or at the very least find it useful. My best wishes for your future success.

Roger Mason

SUNDAY

The right approach

During the rest of the week we will be examining in detail various aspects of accounts. We will see how everything fits together and hopefully understand the bigger picture. We will aim to know what everything means and how to interpret the information. It is quite a challenge and we will get the best results if we approach it in the right way. Furthermore, we need to know about the many problems and traps that await us. So we will spend today preparing for what lies ahead. Our time will not be wasted.

The various aspects that we examine comprise:

The approaches most likely to get the best results

- Look for trends
- Look for reasons
- Be open-minded
- Make comparisons
- Do not neglect the notes and the accounting policies
- Sometimes be suspicious

Traps to avoid

- Applying percentages to small base figures
- Failure to take account of a change in accounting policy
- Not always comparing like with like
- Forgetting that some things can only be known by insiders
- Not taking account of different lengths in the trading period
- Forgetting the effects of inflation
- Not taking account of seasonal factors
- Being misled by averages
- Not realizing that the figures have been manipulated
- Failure to take full account of the notes and other information

SUNDAY

MONDAY

TUESDAY

WEDNESDAY

THURSDAY

FRIDAY

SATURDAY

The approaches most likely to get the best results

The right attitudes are some of those most likely to be displayed by a successful businessman or businesswoman, or indeed by persons successful in many other fields. You are advised to prepare yourself and give the job the necessary time and resources. You should be knowledgeable and cool, calm and collected. It is necessary to be determined and sometimes to be sceptical. At times you must be relentless. The following techniques and attitudes may be particularly helpful.

Look for trends

It is often very useful to examine trends because they may be much more revealing than a single figure or comparison. If you only have one year's accounts or accounts for some other single period, this will not be possible. However, at least for an established business, you will often have the figures for several periods. In the UK, companies are required to publish the figures for the previous period alongside the figures for the current period, so you will always have at least two figures or ratios to compare. The published accounts of

UK listed companies are required to give key data over the previous five years.

A deteriorating payment performance, for example, often indicates liquidity problems, although it can also mean that selfish managers are hoarding cash at the expense of suppliers. If a company has gone from paying in 30 days to paying in 90 days, it may be more worrying than if it has consistently taken 90 days to pay.

Look for reasons

There may be special reasons that should be taken into account when the significance of a ratio is assessed. For example, very high expenditure on advertising right at the end of the financial period may reduce profits for the period, but hold out the promise of higher sales and profits in the next period. Of course, the extra sales and profits might not actually happen. Lord Leverhulme, the founder of Unilever, famously remarked that he knew that half of his company's massive expenditure on advertising was wasted, but he did not know which half.

Be open-minded

You will often approach the task of interpreting accounts with some preconceived ideas about what you will find and what your conclusions will be. This is inevitable and often your preconceived ideas will be correct, but you should never close your mind to the possibility that you will be wrong. Always look at the evidence and make up your mind accordingly.

Make comparisons

A close examination of a set of accounts will give you much information and it might tell you what you want to know. For example, you may be particularly interested in the ratio between net profit and turnover, which is one of the easier calculations to make. If this really is all that you want you can stop at this point, but it will very probably be revealing to compare the ratio that you have obtained with such things as:

- Last year's results
- The budget
- The industry or sector average
- The accounts of a competitor

An apparently successful result might not look so good if it lags behind the competition, the budget and last year's figures. The opposite of course also applies.

Do not neglect the notes and the accounting policies

The figures in the financial statements are the starting point, but only the starting point. A full understanding requires a close study of the notes and the accounting policies. This really does matter.

You may be familiar with the saying 'The large print giveth and the small print taketh away'. Professional analysts always spend time studying the notes to published accounts and the accounting policies. You should do the same and you should pay particular attention to any change in accounting policies. Laws and accounting standards govern certain information that must be disclosed in the notes to published accounts of companies and also in the directors' report.

Sometimes be suspicious

Most (but not all) directors, accountants and business people are reasonably honest, which is just as well, and most of them try to present a good set of accounts that comply with the law, accounting standards and the underlying facts. Furthermore, the tax authorities and in some cases auditors are on hand to fortify their resolve. Many people are of the view that standards are higher in the UK than in many other countries. Nevertheless, a few are dishonest and some others try to show a particular result, so long as a case can be made within the rules for doing so. Still more make honest mistakes.

You can usually trust the integrity of those presenting the accounts, but not always. Perhaps the best approach is that of an old-fashioned bank manager, a species sadly now not often encountered. Ask searching questions of the figures and perhaps of the people who produced them. Do not be easily fooled. If something seems not to be right, perhaps it is not right, even if you are not an expert. Do not give up, and get to the bottom of whatever it is that concerns you.

Traps to avoid

Even experienced financial analysts can make mistakes and fall into one of the many traps that may be encountered, and it is more likely that someone not financially sophisticated will do so. To be forewarned is to be forearmed. The following are some of the more common mistakes.

Applying percentages to small base figures

David Lloyd George, a former British Prime Minister, once asked a civil servant to produce some statistics. The civil servant replied 'Certainly – what would you like me to prove?'. Statistics and ratios can be misleading, especially when small base figures are used. This is best illustrated with an example.

	Turnover £	Profit Before Tax £
Company A		
Year 1	1,000,000	100
Year 2	1,000,000	200
Company B		
Year 1	1,000,000	100,000
Year 2	1,000,000	101,000

Hasn't Company A done well? It has doubled its profit. Poor old Company B, on the other hand, has only managed a miserable 1 per cent increase, but of course this is a ludicrous conclusion to draw. On an identical turnover, Company B has increased its profit by £1,000, whereas Company A has only done so by £100. What is more, Company A is still virtually breaking even, but Company B is making a healthy profit.

Failure to take account of a change in accounting policy

A change in accounting policy may affect the figures and ratios, without there being any change in the underlying reality. The result will be the same in the long run but, as the great economist John Maynard Keynes once said 'In the long run we are all dead'. You will most likely be looking at the figures in the short run, probably a period of a year.

Examples include changes in depreciation policy and changes in the way that stock is valued. The profit is the same in the long term, but the declared profit will be different in the year that the change is made. Fortunately, notes to the published accounts of companies must disclose significant changes in accounting policies and spell out the consequences.

Consider a company that two years ago purchased a piece of machinery for £500,000 and in the first year depreciated it by

25 per cent. In the second year the company changed its policy and depreciated it by 20 per cent. Clearly, the declared net profit before tax will be £25,000 higher than if the change had not been made.

Not always comparing like with like

The most recent (at the time of writing) accounts of Marks and Spencer Group plc disclose the following:

Sales for year (in £ million)	9,934.3
Trade receivables (in £ million)	114.6

You can easily work out that customers take an average of 4.2 days to pay for their purchases. The calculation is:

$$\frac{114.6}{9,934.3} \times 365 = 4.2 \text{ days}$$

You may think that this is stunningly good, and that the company must employ the world's best credit controllers. This may or may not be true, but it should not be deduced from these figures. The reason for this is that the company is in the retail sector and the great majority of its sales are made for cash. Trade receivables should really be compared with just the part of sales that are made on credit.

Now consider a hypothetical widget manufacturer whose accounts disclose the following:

Sales for the year	£900,000
Trade debtors at the balance sheet date	£100,000

This appears to show that customers take an average of 40.6 days to pay. The calculation is:

$$\frac{100,000}{900,000} \times 365 = 40.6 \text{ days}$$

This too is probably wrong because sales will almost certainly exclude VAT, and trade debtors will probably include it. If trade debtors all include 20 per cent VAT, the correct calculation is:

$$\frac{83,333}{900,000} \times 365 = 33.8 \text{ days}$$

83,333 is 100,000 with the 20 per cent VAT removed.

SUNDAY

MONDAY

TUESDAY

WEDNESDAY

THURSDAY

FRIDAY

SATURDAY

Forgetting that some things can only be known by insiders

Published financial statements reveal a great deal, but there are some details that can really only be known by those with inside information. Consider two companies that manufacture and sell screws:

	Company A	Company B
Sales	£3,900,000	£3,700,000
Cost of sales	£2,184,000	£2,146,000
Gross margin	44%	42%

Company A appears to be slightly more efficient, but the figures could be affected by the different accounting treatment of certain factory costs, such as power and property costs. Company A might treat these costs as general overheads, whereas Company B might allocate them to production costs. Overall net profit for the whole company would of course be unaffected.

If you are an insider yourself, you may have all the information that you need, or at least be in a position to get it. If, on the other hand, you are not able to do this, a touch of caution should not come amiss. The problem is much smaller than in the past because accounting standards and more prescriptive laws have reduced the uncertainty, but there are still some things that only an insider can know.

Not taking account of different lengths in the trading period

Consider the following:

	10 months to 31 October	14 months to 31st December in the following year
Sales in period	£6,000,000	£8,400,000
Net profit before tax	£720,000	£1,008,000

Although the second period seems better, if you allow for the different lengths, the results are identical, with the profit percentage being 12 per cent in each case.

This is so conspicuous that you would have to be asleep on the job to miss the significance of the different lengths in the trading period, but the difference might not be so obvious. Most companies prepare annual accounts for an exact calendar year of 52 weeks and 1 day (52 weeks and 2 days in a leap year) but a few make it exactly 52 weeks with an occasional 53-week year to come back into line. This is disclosed, but it does make a difference and its significance can easily be missed. The following are the turnover figures for a very well-known company for three successive years.

	£m
Year 1 (52 weeks)	9,062.1
Year 2 (53 weeks)	9,536.6
Year 3 (52 weeks)	9,740.3

Turnover increased by 5.23 per cent in year 2, but a 53-week year is 1.92 per cent longer than a 52-week year, so more than a third of the increase was down to it being a longer year. It works the other way in year 3. Turnover is up by 2.13 per cent, but if we add the effect of the shorter year it is just over 4 per cent.

Forgetting the effects of inflation

It is sometimes said that carbon monoxide is the silent killer, which is why I have a carbon monoxide alarm in my house. In the same way, inflation is the silent destroyer of value. There have only been two years since 1945 when there has been nil inflation in Britain. Sometimes it is high, as when it peaked at 27.9 per cent in the 1970s, and in many years it is relatively low, but it is almost always there.

The significance of inflation should not be overlooked especially when comparing figures from different periods. The effects are cumulative and it does many things. These include devaluing savings and favouring borrowing. This is because repayments are made in less valuable money. It is a main reason why the baby boomer generation did so well by borrowing to buy property that increased in value in most years.

For a minor example of the effects of inflation you might like to look back to the previous section of this chapter. You will see that the adjusted increase in turnover between years 2 and 3 was just over 4 per cent. The figures are real and inflation was around 4 per cent at that time. After allowing for inflation there was really no increase at all.

Not taking account of seasonal factors

This is a common mistake. Consider Mr Khan who starts selling ice cream from a van on 1st October. Information from his first two six-monthly profit statements is shown below.

	6 months to 31st March	6 months to 30th September
Sales in period	£12,400	£37,200
Net profit before tax	£4,216	£12,276
Profit as a percentage of sales	34%	33%

At first glance this shows that the second period is much better than the first, but this might not be the case, although further investigation may show that there was some improvement. The reason for this conclusion is that the sale of ice cream from vans in Britain is heavily affected by the weather and the amount of daylight. Sales should be much higher in the summer months.

Being misled by averages

A man stood with one leg in a bucket of ice and the other in a bucket of boiling water, so on average he was comfortable. It is a good joke, at least in my opinion, and it is relevant to this book. Averages can be misleading and you may need to get behind the figures that contribute to them.

A holding company had two subsidiaries. The first one made a million pound profit and the second one made a million pound loss. So on average they broke even and this is the result shown in the holding company's group accounts. You obviously need to get behind the group accounts (which are correct) in order to understand what has happened.

Not realizing that the figures have been manipulated

This may have been done within the rules. Consider a company that usually operates with a bank overdraft. However, the managers do not pay suppliers in the last three weeks of the trading period in order to show no bank borrowings in the balance sheet. This is unfair to suppliers, but a common practice. The balance sheet will of course show trade creditors being higher than usual. The opposite practice may also be encountered. This is paying suppliers just before the balance sheet date in order to establish a false, or at least untypical, record for paying suppliers promptly. An even more dubious practice is to draw the cheques just before the balance sheet date but not release them for some time.

Failure to take full account of the notes and other information

It is sometimes said that professional analysts spend more time studying the notes to the accounts than they spend studying the actual accounts. This could be wise of them because the accounts are often just the starting point. As already mentioned, in the UK (as in nearly all other countries) the law and various accounting standards specify a great deal of information that must be disclosed in the notes to the published accounts.

SUNDAY
MONDAY
TUESDAY
WEDNESDAY
THURSDAY
FRIDAY
SATURDAY

Summary

Today we have:

● Seen how we are most likely to get good results and the best rewards for our time and effort if we proceed in the right way. To this end we have looked at a number of attitudes and mindsets that should be brought to bear on the tasks ahead.

● Understood that our work might not be straightforward and that there are traps that could stop us getting the best results. We have studied ten of these traps and resolved to avoid them.

Tomorrow we will learn about accounting standards and see how accounts can be obtained. We will then have a first look at the different types of account and how they are made up.

SUNDAY

MONDAY

TUESDAY

WEDNESDAY

THURSDAY

FRIDAY

SATURDAY

Fact-check (answers at the back)

1. For how many years must the accounts of UK listed companies reveal key data?
   a) Three years ❏
   b) Four years ❏
   c) Five years ❏
   d) Six years ❏

2. With what might it be revealing to compare a company's accounts?
   a) Last year's results ❏
   b) The industry or sector average ❏
   c) The accounts of a competitor ❏
   d) All of the above ❏

3. Who said 'In the long run we are all dead'?
   a) Milton Friedman ❏
   b) Milton Keynes ❏
   c) Maynard Keynes ❏
   d) Bill Maynard ❏

4. Sales for the year are £4,021,626. Amount owing by customers at the year end is £469,318. What is the average period of credit taken by customers?
   a) 37.3 days ❏
   b) 42.6 days ❏
   c) 48.1 days ❏
   d) 55.0 days ❏

5. Which is the factor in Question 4 that might invalidate the answer?
   a) VAT may be in the sales figure but not the amount owing by customers ❏
   b) VAT may be in the amount owing by customers but not in the sales figure ❏
   c) The business might not be registered for VAT ❏
   d) The VAT return is overdue ❏

6. The previous year's profit was £100,000. This year's profit was £102,000. Inflation in the last year was 2 per cent. How have we done in real terms?
   a) Better ❏
   b) Worse ❏
   c) The same ❏
   d) There is not enough information to answer the question ❏

7. A company that has an overdraft does not pay its suppliers in the month before the financial year end. What effect will this have in the balance sheet?
   a) There will be no change ❏
   b) It will increase both creditors and debtors ❏
   c) It will increase the overdraft and the amount owing to creditors ❏
   d) It will reduce the overdraft and increase the amount owing to creditors ❏

8. Does a deteriorating payment performance always indicate that a customer has liquidity problems?
a) Yes, always ☐
b) No, never ☐
c) No, but it often does ☐
d) Only if it is around the Christmas period ☐

9. Is it a good idea to examine trends in the accounts?
a) Yes ☐
b) No ☐
c) Only if you are not busy ☐
d) It is positively harmful ☐

10. Who said that he knew that half of his company's massive expenditure on advertising was wasted, but he did not know which half?
a) Robert Maxwell ☐
b) Lord Leverhulme ☐
c) Lord Sugar ☐
d) Sir Richard Branson ☐

MONDAY

An introduction to accounts

It is now time to get started. An introduction to accounts means first of all knowing how to get hold of accounts and, although you may well already know what they look like, you need to know something about accounting standards and what exactly comprises a package of financial statements and reports. We will then, during the rest of the week, be able to set about examining, interpreting and understanding them, but first of all, today, you will be introduced to them.

The topics covered today comprise:

- An example of unpublished accounts
- How to obtain copies of published accounts
- Accounting standards
- Accounts prepared in accordance with UK accounting standards
- Accounts prepared in accordance with international accounting standards
- Abbreviated accounts of small and medium-sized companies
- Audit

An example of unpublished accounts

Unpublished accounts do not have to comply with laws and accounting standards, and they are not audited. You should bear this in mind. They are usually prepared by managers for managers and can be laid out in the way that they think most suits their purposes. They are often prepared monthly or quarterly so that managers can monitor progress. There will be a profit and loss account and perhaps a balance sheet. The profit and loss account is likely to be accompanied by a listing of the expenses and a comparison with the budget. A typical profit and loss account might be as follows.

XYZ Ltd

Profit and Loss Account for the 3 Months to 31st March

	£	£
Sales		1,021,429
Stock at 31st December	326,491	
Add purchases	489,617	
	816,108	
Less stock at 31st March	299,998	
		516,110
		505,319
Less overheads		
Sales department	84,116	
Finance department	96,238	
Administration department	187,205	
		367,559
Net profit before tax		137,760

The same company's balance sheet at 31st March could be as follows

XYZ Ltd

Balance Sheet at 31st March

	£	£
Fixed assets		
Freehold property	590,000	
Computers	32,191	
Motor vehicles	22,478	
		644,669
Current assets		
Stock	299,998	
Trade debtors	87,172	
Cash in bank	63,491	
	450,661	
Less current liabilities		
Trade creditors	102,345	
Other creditors	58,991	
	161,336	
Net current assets		289,325
		933,994
Capital		
Share capital		500,000
Revenue reserve		433,994
		933,994

At this point would you please look at the accounts and draw some conclusions, bearing in mind of course the possible traps mentioned yesterday, and that they are unpublished and unaudited. Having said that, I would be disappointed if you did not spot at least the following two things:

1 The direct cost of goods sold is 50.5 per cent, which may or may not be good according to circumstances. The calculation is:

$$\frac{516,110}{1,021,429} \times 100 = 50.5 \text{ per cent}$$

2 The company appears to be profitable and well financed. On this information at least, the risk of it failing would appear to be small.

How to obtain copies of published accounts

You may already have the accounts that you want. Furthermore, you may have the right to be sent copies for a particular company or other body. For example, in the UK all shareholders can require (request would be more polite) that a copy of the latest accounts be sent to them without charge. Members of building societies and other bodies have rights too. However, this section of the chapter explains how you can get copies of accounts and limited liability partnerships from Companies House.

There are more than 2,650,000 companies registered at Companies House and more than 50,000 limited liability partnerships (LLPs). All but a tiny number of unlimited companies are required to file accounts. They must also file an annual return and certain other information. The accounts and the other information are placed on public record and anyone can obtain a copy. You can also get accounts and other documents for previous years. You have this right and you do not have to give a reason.

The most convenient method is likely to be by using the Companies House website www.companieshouse.gov.uk, or alternatively you can ring 0303 1234 500. You will need the company's exact registered name, its registered number, or preferably both. There is a charge of £1 per document (a set of accounts counts as a document) if it is sent electronically, or £3 per document if it is sent by post. Contact details for Companies House are as follows.

Offices in England and Wales	Office in Scotland	Office in Northern Ireland
Crown Way	4th Floor	Second Floor
Maindy	Edinburgh Quay 2	The Linenhall
Cardiff	139 Fountainbridge	32-38 Linenhall Street
CF14 3UZ	Edinburgh	Belfast
Tel 0303 1234 500	EH3 9FF	BT2 8BG
	Tel 0303 1234 500	Tel 0303 1234 500
21 Bloomsbury Street		
London		
WC1B 3XD		
Tel 0303 1234 500		
Website (all offices)	www.companieshouse.gov.uk	

Accounting standards

Accounting standards were introduced in the early 1970s in response to a number of scandals (Pergamon Press was a notable example) and complaints that different companies were (perhaps quite legitimately) using different rules and getting different results. From small beginnings UK standards have grown into a comprehensive body of rules. International accounting standards also comprise a comprehensive body of rules.

Directors have an overall responsibility to ensure that the accounts give a 'true and fair view'. It is not a specific legal requirement that accounts conform with accounting standards. However, accounts almost always do conform with accounting standards. This is partly because accounting standards are generally respected, partly because failure to comply would generate suspicious questions and partly because it would result in a qualified audit report. Very occasionally directors do

SUNDAY
MONDAY
TUESDAY
WEDNESDAY
THURSDAY
FRIDAY
SATURDAY

deviate from accounting standards and give their reasons for doing so, which is permitted.

It is a requirement that a statement be given in the notes to the accounts as to whether the accounts have been prepared in accordance with applicable accounting standards. It requires particulars of any material departure from the standards and the reasons for the departure to be given.

International accounting standards are issued by the International Accounting Standards Board and, as the name implies, are intended to be used internationally. Listed companies within the European Union are required to comply with international accounting standards, though UK listed companies may use UK standards for their subsidiary companies if they wish. Alternative Investment Market (AIM) listed companies count as listed companies for this purpose. Other UK companies can decide to use international standards if they wish, but having done so they can never return to UK standards unless their circumstances change.

Accounts prepared in accordance with UK accounting standards

The following are required if UK GAAP (generally accepted accounting principles) are used:

- A balance sheet
- A profit and loss account
- A statement of total recognized gains and losses (STRGL)

If a company revalues its assets, a note of historical cost profits and losses may follow the profit and loss account or the STRGL.

Most companies also include a cash flow statement in their financial statements.

Notes to the financial statements are also required.

Comparable figures for the previous period must in all cases be stated.

The financial statements must be accompanied by a directors' report and, for all but small companies, a business review. A chairman's report is optional.

Space does not permit extensive examples, but the following is a real example of a profit and loss account prepared in accordance with UK GAAP.

	Note	Current Year £	Previous Year £
TURNOVER	2	5,712,480	5,455,154
Cost of sales		905,147	1,331,433
GROSS PROFIT		4,807,333	4,123,721
Distribution costs		144,191	320,025
Administrative expenses		4,302,709	3,543,711
OPERATING PROFIT	3	360,433	259,985
Interest payable and similar charges	5	23,779	15,159
PROFIT ON ORDINARY ACTIVITIES BEFORE TAXATION		336,654	244,826
Tax on profit on ordinary activities		–	–
PROFIT ON ORDINARY ACTIVITIES AFTER TAXATION		336,654	244,826
Extraordinary items	6	–	462,291
PROFIT/LOSS FOR THE FINANCIAL YEAR		336,654	(217,465)
Balance brought forward		(1,801,285)	(1,583,820)
Balance carried forward		(1,464,631)	(1,801,285)

All of the activities of the company are classed as continuing.

The company has no recognized gains or losses other than the results for the year as set out above.

Accounts prepared in accordance with international accounting standards

The following are required if international accounting standards are used:

● An income statement immediately followed by a statement of comprehensive income (SORIE) or a single statement of comprehensive income which combines the income statement and the SORIE

- A statement of financial position (this is the revised name for the balance sheet and it is still permitted to use the term balance sheet instead)
- A statement of changes in equity
- A statement of cash flows
- Notes to the financial statements

Comparable figures for the previous period must in all cases be stated.

The financial statements must be accompanied by a directors' report and for all but small companies a business review. In the case of a listed company a chairman's report and a directors' remuneration report are required.

Abbreviated accounts of small and medium-sized companies

In the UK, small and medium-sized companies may prepare abbreviated accounts for Companies House, though they must send full accounts to their members (this usually means their shareholders). There are a few exceptions but otherwise the definitions are:

Small company

A company that on a group basis satisfies any two of the following three conditions for both the current financial year and the previous financial year:

- Turnover not more than £6,500,000
- Balance sheet total not more than £3,260,000
- Average number of employees not more than 50

Medium-sized company

A company that on a group basis satisfies any two of the following three conditions for both the current financial year and the previous financial year:

- Turnover not more than £25,900,000
- Balance sheet total not more than £12,900,000
- Average number of employees not more than 250

The privilege of abbreviated accounts relates to accounts sent to the Registrar of Companies, and are thus placed on public record. It does not apply to the accounts that must be sent to company members. A company need not take advantage of any or all of the privileges of abbreviated accounts.

The privileges of small and medium-sized accounts are as follows:

Small company

- No profit and loss account is necessary
- No directors' report is necessary
- The balance sheet and notes may be in summarized form

Medium-sized company

Certain information relating to the profit and loss account need not be disclosed. In particular, it is not necessary to show other operating income and cost of sales. The balance sheet and notes must be shown in full. Medium-sized companies are required to disclose their turnover.

Small and medium-sized companies do not have to take advantage of any or all of these privileges but most of them do. Analysing small and medium-sized companies' abbreviated accounts is frustrating because of the lack of information. This is particularly true of small companies.

Audit

An audit is compulsory for a company unless it meets all of the following criteria:

- It is a private company
- It is a small company as defined in this chapter
- Balance sheet total is not more than £3,260,000
- Turnover is not more than £6,500,000
- It is not part of a group that is required to prepare audited accounts

There are one or two exceptions such as banking companies.

This is for accounts periods ending on or before 30th September 2012. There are changes for accounts periods ending after this date.

The auditor has a number of responsibilities, including stating in the audit report an opinion as to whether or not the financial statements give a 'true and fair view'. The auditor does not certify the figures, a point which is frequently misunderstood.

Summary

We have done a lot today. We have:

- Seen an example of unpublished accounts, the sort that you might see during the year in the course of your employment.
- Noted how to obtain copies of the published accounts of registered companies and limited liability partnerships.
- Discovered why accounting standards are so important in understanding and interpreting accounts.
- Found out more about accounts prepared in accordance with both UK accounting standards and international accounting standards.
- Looked at the definition of small and medium-sized companies for accounting purposes and seen how their accounts need to provide less information.
- Had a brief introduction to the subject of audit.

Tomorrow we start examining the accounts in detail starting with the one that many people turn to first. This is the profit and loss account, which will be called the income statement if international accounting statements have been used.

SUNDAY

MONDAY

TUESDAY

WEDNESDAY

THURSDAY

FRIDAY

SATURDAY

Fact-check (answers at the back)

1. Must unpublished accounts comply with accounting standards?
   a) Yes ☐
   b) No ☐
   c) Only if the accounts are for a company that is insolvent ☐
   d) Only if it is a listed company ☐

2. Which of general partnerships and limited liability partnerships are required to file accounts at Companies House?
   a) Both general partnerships and limited liability partnerships ☐
   b) Neither general partnerships nor limited liability partnerships ☐
   c) Just general partnerships ☐
   d) Just limited liability partnerships ☐

3. Can you get copies of accounts for previous years from Companies House?
   a) Yes ☐
   b) No ☐
   c) Only if you pay more ☐
   d) Only for the previous three years ☐

4. What is the charge for obtaining a set of accounts from Companies House?
   a) £10 ☐
   b) £1 ☐
   c) £3 ☐
   d) £1 if provided electronically, but £3 if provided by post ☐

5. Must AIM listed companies use international accounting standards?
   a) Yes ☐
   b) No ☐
   c) Only if they have never used UK standards ☐
   d) Only if the company is less than five years old ☐

6. Must the accounts of public companies be audited?
   a) Yes ☐
   b) No ☐
   c) Only if turnover is more than £6,500,000 ☐
   d) Only if they are listed on a stock exchange ☐

7. What name is used for the profit and loss account if international accounting standards are used?
   a) Profit statement ☐
   b) Profit or loss statement ☐
   c) Income statement ☐
   d) Statement of surplus or deficit ☐

8. Using either UK accounting standards or international accounting standards, for how many previous periods must comparable figures be stated?
   a) One previous period ☐
   b) Two previous periods ☐
   c) Three previous periods ☐
   d) Four previous periods ☐

9. For whom or what must small companies provide a profit and loss account?
a) Just Companies House ❏
b) Just their members (this usually means shareholders) ❏
c) Both Companies House and their members ❏
d) Neither Companies House nor their members ❏

10. Does an auditor certify the accuracy of the financial statements?
a) Yes ❏
b) No ❏
c) Only if it is a public company ❏
d) Only if it is for the first accounting period of a newly registered company ❏

SUNDAY MONDAY TUESDAY WEDNESDAY THURSDAY FRIDAY SATURDAY

TUESDAY

The profit and loss account or income statement

If you studied yesterday's chapter carefully you will know why what most people instinctively call the profit and loss account is sometimes called the income statement. Why did they have to change the term? In the words of the hymn 'Change and decay in all around I see'.

The first financial statement that we study in detail is the one that most people turn to first. Many consider it to be the most important. We will see what the profit and loss account is and what it does, and we will see how it is laid out, conforming with each of the two sets of accounting standards. We will look at the long list of information that must be disclosed in the notes and, finally and very importantly, we will do some relevant analysis work.

The topics covered today comprise:

- What is a profit and loss account or income statement?
- Extra factors for trading and manufacturing businesses
- Income statement prepared in accordance with international accounting standards (IFRS)
- Profit and loss account prepared in accordance with UK accounting standards (UK GAAP)
- SORIE and STRGL
- Information that must be given
- Some useful analysis

What is a profit and loss account or income statement?

A profit and loss account or income statement is a summary of the accounts of an income and expense nature in the bookkeeping system. Invoiced sales and rental income are examples of accounts of an income nature, and salaries and advertising costs are examples of accounts of an expenditure nature. The difference between the total of the income accounts and the total of the expenditure accounts is the profit or loss for the period.

The heading of the profit and loss account or income statement must state the period of time that it covers. This is often a year, but could be some other period. It is important to understand that it is a summary of activity over a period of time. So, for example, if in the course of a year 10,000 invoices to customers have been issued and they total 6 million pounds, it is 6 million pounds that will appear in the profit and loss account. This is fundamentally different from a balance sheet which lists assets and liabilities as at a stated date, not activity over a period of time.

It is obviously important that accounts be properly classified, as a mistake can distort the figures. For example, if an account of an expenditure nature (such as the costs of running company cars) is classed as an asset (such as the purchase of company cars) both the profit and the fixed assets in the balance sheet will be overstated.

In published accounts at least, revenue should be sales made outside the group. Whether or not revenue is recognized for the period is a big and contentious subject, with individual decisions being a matter for accounting standards and individual judgement. This can be a factor in such things as major construction projects lasting several years. Whether payment has been received for the sales is not material.

There are only common sense considerations if the profit and loss account is unpublished and for internal use only, but a published profit and loss account must be laid out in a certain way with required supporting information given in the notes. Specified headings must be used, but they may be omitted if not relevant to a particular profit and loss account or income statement.

Extra factors for trading and manufacturing businesses

If a company sells goods rather than provides services, it is important that its profit and loss account or income statement only includes the cost of goods sold in the period, rather than the cost of goods purchased. The following shows how it is done.

	£	£
Sales		10,000,000
Stock at the beginning of the period	3,000,000	
Add purchases during the period	8,000,000	
	11,000,000	
Less stock at the end of the period	5,000,000	
Cost of goods sold		6,000,000
		4,000,000

It would obviously be a dreadful mistake to say that the cost of goods sold was £8,000,000, being the cost of goods purchased in the period.

The same principle applies in the accounts of a business that manufactures goods. The total manufacturing cost of goods sold in the period must be brought into the profit and loss account or income statement, not the amount spent on manufacturing. The cost of raw materials, bought in components and manufacturing costs for just the goods sold is what is wanted.

Income statement prepared in accordance with international accounting standards (IFRS)

The following is an actual example of an income statement prepared in accordance with international accounting standards. It is for a subsidiary company within a group and it is a very simple and straightforward example. Income statements can be and often are much longer and much more complicated. It is the real income statement of a real company, but we will call it Company A.

Company A

Income Statement for the Year to.....

	Note	Current Year £000	Previous Year £000
Revenue	3	1,604	1,243
Selling and distribution expenses		(52)	(41)
Administrative expenses		(1,386)	(1,134)
Operating profit	4	166	68
Profit before taxation		166	68
Tax expense	7	(46)	(22)
Profit for the year		120	46

Revenue and operating profit is derived entirely from continuing operations.

All profits are attributable to the owners of the company, as there is no non-controlling interest.

The company has no recognized gains or losses for the current or prior year other than those recognized in the company's income statement, hence no statement of comprehensive income is prepared.

Note 3 explains the source of the company's revenue and states how much of it was earned outside the United Kingdom.

Note 4 gives details of certain expenses deducted in arriving at the operating profit.

Note 7 explains in detail the calculation of the taxation charge.

Profit and loss account prepared in accordance with UK accounting standards (UK GAAP)

The following is an actual example of a profit and loss account prepared in accordance with UK accounting standards. It is the real profit and loss account of a real company, but we will call it Company B.

Company B

Profit and Loss Account for the Year to.....

	Note	Current Year £	Previous Year £
Turnover	1	22,680,815	25,792,130
Cost of sales		(12,076,105)	(15,154,851)
Gross profit		10,604,710	10,637,279
		46.8%	41.2%

Distribution costs		(387,026)	(422,807)
Administrative expenses		(11,434,707)	(11,379,665)
Other operating income	3	657,110	334,760
		(11,164,623)	(11,467,712)
Operating loss before amortization of goodwill		(559,913)	(830,433)
Goodwill amortization	8	(267,017)	(298,250)
Operating loss		(826,930)	1,128,683)
Interest receivable and similar income	4	164,819	156,890
Loss on ordinary activities before taxation		(662,111)	(971,793)
Tax on loss on ordinary activities	5	457,126	169,894
Loss on ordinary activities after taxation	19	(204,985)	(801,899)

CONSOLIDATED STATEMENT OF TOTAL RecognizeD GAINS AND LOSSES

	£	£
Loss attributable to shareholders	(204,985)	(726,899)
Unrealized deficit on revaluation of investment properties	–	(75,000)
Total recognized losses since last financial statements	(204,985)	(801,899)

Note 1 is 'turnover and loss on ordinary activities before taxation'. It splits the turnover between sales in the UK and sales overseas, and it details expenditure on:

- Audit services
- Depreciation of tangible fixed assets
- Amortization of intangibles
- Operating lease rentals
- Profit or loss on sale of fixed assets
- Loss on foreign exchange

Note 3 gives details of operating income from sources other than the main business. This includes income from leasing premises.

Note 8 gives further details of goodwill amortization. Goodwill is the amount paid for a business in excess of its book value and it must be amortized (written off) over a number of years.

Note 4 splits the interest receivable between bank interest and other interest.

Note 5 gives details of the tax charge or tax credit. It is a credit in this case because the company has made a significant loss.

Note 19 is headed 'reconciliation of movements in total equity shareholders' funds'. This note relates to the balance sheet as well as the profit and loss account and it shows how the value of the share capital and reserves is affected by the after-tax loss and the payment of dividends.

SORIE and STRGL

We had better start by stating what these acronyms stand for.

SORIE stands for 'statement of recognized income and expense' and this is required if an income statement is prepared using international accounting standards. It must appear under the income statement or be incorporated in a single statement of comprehensive income.

STRGL sounds rather like struggle and it might be a struggle to prepare, but this is not correct. It stands for 'statement of total recognized gains and losses'. It must appear under the profit and loss account if it is prepared using UK accounting standards.

SORIE and STRGL fulfil essentially the same purpose. As already stated in this chapter an income statement and a profit and loss account summarize the accounts in the bookkeeping system of an income and expense nature. The difference between the two totals is the profit or loss for the period. However, under accounting rules some gains and losses go straight to the balance sheet without first passing through the income statement or profit and loss account. In the balance sheet they increase or decrease the value of the business according to whether they are gains or losses.

This is done because the gains or losses are not realized gains or losses. They might not actually happen or, if they do, the realized gains or losses might be for different amounts. Despite this it is considered right to show them in the accounts, which is what SORIE and STRGL do. An example of such an unrealized gain or loss is a revaluation of some of the fixed assets at an amount different from the book value.

The foot of the income statement of Company A, which is shown in this chapter, states that there is nothing to report in a statement of comprehensive income. Company B, whose profit and loss account is also shown in this chapter, had one thing to report in the previous year. Investment properties were valued at £75,000 less than the book value. This shortfall is reflected in the balance sheet but has not passed through the profit and loss account.

The list of factors can be long and technical. The consolidated statement of comprehensive income in the latest accounts of Marks and Spencer Group plc lists the following:

- Foreign currency translation differences
- Actuarial (losses)/gains on retirement benefit schemes
- Tax on retirement benefit schemes
- Cash flow and net investment hedges
- Fair value movements in equity
- Reclassified and reported in net profit
- Amount recognized in inventories
- Tax on cash flow hedges and net investment hedges

It sounds complicated and troublesome and it probably is.

Information that must be given

In the case of a company, the Companies Act and accounting standards require extensive information to be given in the notes. If there is nothing to report under a particular heading, it is not necessary to have that heading in the notes. The following are many of the requirements:

The amount of the company's profit or loss on ordinary activities before taxation

This is 'profit before tax' which is obviously a key figure and probably familiar to you. It is often the first figure in the entire accounts package that users of accounts turn to. Ordinary activities exclude extraordinary income and expenditure, and they also exclude exceptional income and expenditure. These are explained next.

Extraordinary income and expenditure

These are separate from the ordinary activities of the company and must be identified as such. An extreme and unrealistic example is a mining company opening a massage parlour.

Exceptional income and expenditure

These are derived from ordinary activities, but are exceptional because of their size or some other factor. A possible example is significant redundancy and other costs incurred when closing a division or activities at a particular location. It is sometimes said that directors have an incentive to class costs as exceptional in order to make the result of ordinary activities look better. This would be both wrong and hopefully very unusual.

Prior year adjustments

These may be necessitated by the discovery of a fundamental error in previous accounts or by a change in accounting policy. The policy on valuing stocks is a possible example as this affects reported profits.

Interest payable and receivable and similar

Interest payable must be analysed between the following categories:

- Amounts payable on bank loans and overdrafts
- Loans of any other kind made to the company
- Lease finance charges allocated for the year

Gains and losses on the repurchase or early settlement of debt should be separately disclosed as should the unwinding of any discount on provisions.

Income from listed investments

Rent receivable in connection with land

Payments for the hire of plant and machinery

Details of auditors' remuneration

This must be split as follows:

- Remuneration (inclusive of sums paid in respect of expenses)
- The aggregate of other fees paid to the auditors and their associates, with a split showing the categories of services provided
- The nature of any benefit in kind provided to the auditors

Details of turnover

The requirements are quite detailed but, as a minimum, a note must show the breakdown by geographical region and by class of business. The note for Company B, whose profit and loss account was shown earlier in this chapter, states that there was only one class of business. It then gives the following information.

	Current Year £	Previous Year £
Existing operations		
United Kingdom	20,715,244	23,951,158
Overseas	1,965,571	1,840,972
	22,680,815	25,792,130

Employees

The average number of persons employed by the company in the year, determined on a monthly basis, must be shown. There must be an analysis between appropriate categories, as determined by the directors, of the monthly number of employees.

The aggregate amounts for the period must be shown for:

- Wages and salaries
- Social security costs
- Other pension costs

The basis of any foreign currency translation

Details of any transfers to and from reserves

Appropriations (including dividends)

Details must be given of:

- The aggregate amount of dividends paid and proposed
- The amount set aside or proposed to be set aside to, or withdrawn or proposed to be withdrawn, from reserves
- The amounts set aside for redemption of share capital or for redemption of loans
- The aggregate of dividends for each class of share
- The amount of any appropriation of profits in respect of non-equity shares other than dividends

Government grants

The effect of government grants on the results for the period must be shown.

Capitalization, depreciation, amortization and impairment

The requirements are quite lengthy and detailed.

Directors' remuneration

There are separate and much greater requirements for quoted companies, but the following must be given for other companies:

- Amounts paid to or receivable by directors in respect of qualifying services
- Amounts paid to or receivable by directors in respect of long-term incentive schemes
- Any company contributions paid to pension schemes

The following must be disclosed if the aggregate directors' emoluments are £200,000 or higher:

- The emoluments of the highest paid director
- The value of the company contributions paid, or treated as paid, to a money purchase pension scheme in respect of the highest paid director
- Where the highest paid director is a member of a defined benefit pension scheme, and has performed pensionable qualifying services in the year
  a) the amount at the end of the year of his/her accrued pension
  b) the amount at the end of the year of his/her accrued lump sum
- If the highest paid director exercised any share options in the year, then a statement of this fact
- If the highest paid director received, or became entitled to receive, any shares under a long-term incentive scheme, then a statement of that fact

Pension costs
Taxation
An analysis of tax payable must be given. There are lengthy detailed requirements.

Some useful analysis

Following are three very common and useful examples of ratio analysis that can be applied to a profit and loss account and supporting notes:

Profit to turnover

This is possibly the simplest of the ratios and one of the most commonly used. It is profit expressed as a percentage of turnover in the year. Sometimes profit before interest payable is used. Sometimes it is profit before tax and sometimes it is profit after tax. As with all the ratios you are free to use the definition that best suits your purposes. The turnover figure does not change of course.

Company A did not pay any interest in the year so interest is not relevant in this case. Using profit before tax the percentage is:

$$\frac{166}{1,604} \times 100 = 10.3 \text{ per cent.}$$

Is this good or not? It sounds all right and it probably is all right, but we do not really know. We need to ask questions such as:

● What was expected?
● What was the budget?
● How did the competition do?
● Are there any special factors that should be taken into account?
● What sort of business is the company in?

Company B made a loss both before and after tax. The tax figure is actually a credit because of the loss. Despite this, the company is well funded and because of excellent profits in earlier years it has a secure balance sheet, as we will see when we look at it tomorrow. It had no need to borrow and in fact there was interest receivable. Using the figure for the operating loss, the loss to turnover percentage is:

$$\frac{826,930}{22,680,815} \times 100 = 3.6 \text{ per cent.}$$

At least it was better than in the previous year.

This accounting ratio is often quoted by people who say 'Look after the top line and the bottom line will look after itself'. There can be an element of truth in this but there are inherent flaws, as you will find if you consistently sell goods at below cost price. Buying turnover at the expense of margins might not be a good idea.

Gross profit margin

In a manufacturing or trading business, gross profit (or gross loss) is the difference between sales and the cost of manufacturing or buying the products sold. In a service business it is the difference between sales and the direct cost of providing the service. In both cases overheads are excluded from the calculation.

Gross margin is particularly important in many businesses because cost of sales is usually by far the biggest cost. If the cost of sales can be reduced by a few percentage points, it can have a big impact on net profit on the bottom line. British supermarkets are just one example of businesses that work hard, and often successfully, to hold down the cost of sales and maintain a satisfactory gross profit margin.

It is not a legal requirement that the gross profit percentage be stated in the accounts, but Company B very helpfully states on the face of the profit and loss account that it is 46.8 per cent. This means that the cost of sales is 53.2 per cent. Is this good? Once again it all depends. Some businesses have a policy of seeking high margins, even at the expense of turnover. Other businesses do the opposite. To use the well-known phrase, they 'pile it high and sell it cheap'. What is best depends on many factors, including the policy of the competition.

Interest cover

This is an important and much-studied ratio, especially when borrowing is high relative to shareholders' funds. This situation, known as being highly geared, is explained later in the week. It is also particularly significant when the interest charge is high relative to profits. Obviously a company that cannot pay its interest charge has severe problems and might not be able to carry on, at least not without a fresh injection of funds.

Interest cover is profit before interest and tax divided by the interest charge. The higher the resulting number the more easily the business is managing to pay the interest charge. The following is an example of the calculation:

	£000
Interest	814
Operating profit	8,698
Interest cover	10.7 times

This is obviously not a problem, and companies A and B, whose details were given earlier, are still better placed because they have no interest charge at all. But what about this?

	£000
Interest	719
Operating profit	790
Interest cover	1.1 times

This is worrying and there are questions to be answered.

Summary

Today we have had a close look at the profit and loss account (or income statement). In particular we have:

- Seen the purpose of the profit and loss account and seen examples of how it is laid out, using both international and UK standards. We have also seen what supporting information must be provided in the notes.
- Looked at the statement of recognized income and expense (SORIE) and the statement of total recognized gains and losses (STRGL). We have seen how they record unrealized gains and losses not recorded in the profit and loss account.
- Been introduced to three regularly used accounting ratios that are used in connection with profit and loss accounts.

Tomorrow we will move on to the balance sheet (which might be called the statement of financial position). This is usually regarded as the second main component of the financial statements and it is fundamentally different from the profit and loss account. Our approach will be similar to the approach that we have adopted today.

SUNDAY
MONDAY
TUESDAY
WEDNESDAY
THURSDAY
FRIDAY
SATURDAY

Fact-check (answers at the back)

1. What must be stated in the heading of a profit and loss account?
   a) Whether it complies with the law ❑
   b) Whether it applies with accounting standards ❑
   c) The period of time that it covers ❑
   d) Whether it has been audited ❑

2. What is the consequence if an account of an expenditure nature is wrongly classed as a fixed asset?
   a) Both the profit and the fixed assets in the balance sheet will be overstated ❑
   b) Both the profit and the fixed assets in the balance sheet will be understated ❑
   c) Both income and expenditure in the profit and loss account will be overstated ❑
   d) The increase in the fixed assets will be compensated by an increase in the depreciation charge ❑

3. Stock at 31st December is £400,000. Purchases in the six months to 30th June are £1,600,000. Stock at 30th June is £600,000. What is the cost of sales for the six months to 30th June?
   a) £1,600,000 ❑
   b) £1,400,000 ❑
   c) £400,000 ❑
   d) £600,000 ❑

4. Which phrase best sums up the purpose of the statement of recognized income and expense (SORIE)?
   a) It is an essential step in making the balance sheet balance ❑
   b) It repeats the most important elements of the income statement ❑
   c) It summarizes the income and expenditure ❑
   d) It states unrealized gains and losses that have passed to the balance sheet without affecting the income statement ❑

5. Which phrase best sums up 'exceptional income and expenditure'?
   a) They are separate from the ordinary activities of the company ❑
   b) They are derived from ordinary activities, but are exceptional because of their size or some other factor ❑
   c) They are exceptionally large ❑
   d) They are exceptionally important ❑

6. Where must the breakdown of turnover by geographical region be shown?
   a) In the balance sheet ❑
   b) In the profit and loss account ❑
   c) In the directors' report ❑
   d) In the notes ❑

7. When must the term 'income statement' be used?
a) When international accounting standards are used ☐
b) When UK accounting standards are used ☐
c) When it is a listed company ☐
d) When it is a small or medium-sized company ☐

8. Turnover is £1,000,000, profit before tax is £100,000 and profit after tax is £79,000. What is the profit after tax to turnover percentage?
a) 10.0 per cent ☐
b) 9.0 per cent ☐
c) 7.9 per cent ☐
d) 8.5 per cent ☐

9. Turnover is £10,000,000 and the gross profit margin is 36.3 per cent. Is this good?
a) Yes ☐
b) No ☐
c) Perhaps ☐
d) Only if the company is in the retail sector ☐

10. Interest payable is £1,264,000 and the operating profit is £7,388,000. What is the interest cover?
a) 4.8 times ☐
b) 5.8 times ☐
c) It is not covered ☐
d) 9.1 times ☐

WEDNESDAY

The balance sheet or statement of financial position

The balance sheet is usually regarded as one of the two main financial statements and it is our task to thoroughly understand it. We will study what it is, what it is for and how it is laid out. This will be when it is an internal document prepared for management, when it is prepared in accordance with international accounting standards and when it is prepared in accordance with UK accounting standards.

We will see what is meant by the main balance sheet headings and see what information must be disclosed in the notes to a published balance sheet.

The topics covered today comprise:

- What is a balance sheet or statement of financial position?
- The concept of ownership
- The layout of the balance sheet
- The main balance sheet headings
- Statement of financial position (or balance sheet) prepared in accordance with international financial standards (IFRS)
- Balance sheet prepared in accordance with UK accounting standards
- Information that must be given

SUNDAY MONDAY TUESDAY WEDNESDAY THURSDAY FRIDAY SATURDAY

What is a balance sheet or statement of financial position?

A balance sheet or statement of financial position is very different from a profit and loss account or income statement. These summarize income and expenditure over a period, the difference between total income and total expenditure being the profit or loss. A balance sheet or statement of financial position, on the other hand, is a listing of the assets and liabilities in a logical way as at a stated date. You can help yourself remember this by thinking of the literal meaning of the words 'balance' and 'sheet'.

Balance

This means that the balance sheet must balance, which is another way of saying that the total of the assets must equal the total of the liabilities.

Sheet

Taken literally this means a sheet of paper on which the figures are listed.

A balance sheet is virtually always dated the last day of the profit and loss account period. The profit from the profit and loss account is transferred to the balance sheet, which ensures that it balances. If the balance sheet (or statement of financial position) is published, the corresponding figures from the previous balance sheet (which will be dated the last day of the previous profit and loss period) must be given.

Another analogy which you might find helpful is to think of a balance sheet as a freeze-frame picture. It summarizes the assets and liabilities on a fixed date. If the date were to be one day earlier or one day later, the figures would be different.

The concept of ownership

Asset and liability accounts are relatively easy to understand, but the capital accounts may cause difficulties. Sometimes there may be just one account called the capital account. In other cases there may be several accounts. Examples in a company are:

- Share capital account
- Share premium account
- Revenue reserves

The capital accounts represent the net worth of the business. This is the present book value of the owners' investment in the business, which is not the same thing as the amount of their original investment. The owners are a different entity to the business itself. A registered company has a legal existence and personality separate from the shareholders who own it. This is not the case in a business owned by a sole trader, but in bookkeeping and accounting practice a sole trader's business is distinct from the sole trader personally. It follows that the net assets of a business owned by a sole trader are owing to the sole trader.

If a company is wound up, and if the assets and liabilities are worth book value and if the costs of winding up are ignored, the owners will be paid out exactly the value of the capital accounts. This is easy to understand in the case of a listed public company. If you own shares in Barclays Bank plc, you are not the same as the bank, you are just one of a very large number of its owners. The capital accounts in the books of Barclays Bank plc represent the money owing to you and the other shareholders. It is the value of the combined investment made by all the shareholders.

The capital accounts represent the 'net worth' of the business, which is the difference between the assets and the liabilities. Hopefully, and usually, the assets exceed the liabilities, so 'net worth' is the correct description. If liabilities exceed the assets, the business is insolvent and the 'net worth' is negative.

We have today looked mainly at the accounts of companies but the concept of ownership applies equally to partnerships and even to sole traders.

The layout of the balance sheet

Until the last 50 years or so it was the practice to set out the figures side by side. The assets were listed on the left and the liabilities were listed on the right. This is no longer done and a vertical format is used.

A vertical balance sheet shows the liabilities deducted from the assets in a logical manner. The assets are stated in the order of their permanence, with fixed assets being shown before current assets and the same principle followed within fixed assets. For example, if a business owns freehold land and buildings, this will almost certainly be the most permanent asset. Therefore it is usual to list this first within the category of fixed assets. The assets and liabilities add down to the 'net worth' of the business. The figure for net worth is represented by the capital accounts which are shown separately and have the same total.

This is best illustrated with an example. The following is the balance sheet of a partnership where the two partners share the profits equally:

Smith and Jones

Balance Sheet at 30th April

	£	£
Fixed assets		
Freehold property	200,000	
Plant and machinery	120,000	
Motor vehicles	40,000	
		360,000
Current assets		
Stock	170,000	
Trade debtors	130,000	
	300,000	
Less current liabilities		
Bank overdraft	60,000	
Trade creditors	120,000	
	180,000	
Net current assets		120,000
		480,000
Capital accounts		
Smith		240,000
Jones		240,000
		480,000

This is, of course, a simple balance sheet. In practice there would be several notes giving relevant details of how the figures are made up. Note that the net worth of the partnership is £480,000. If the partnership were to be wound up, if the assets and liabilities achieved book value and if there were no winding up expenses, Smith and Jones would each get £240,000.

The main balance sheet headings

Of course, not every individual account in the bookkeeping system appears individually in the balance sheet. If it did, the balance sheet of a major company would be hundreds of pages long. The need for this is overcome by grouping accounts of a similar type. For example, the business may owe money to many suppliers, but just one figure for the total will appear in the balance sheet as 'trade creditors'.

An explanation of the main terms used in balance sheets follows. Particular terms are specified by accounting standards, but the following should be very helpful and some of them can be seen in the balance sheet of Smith and Jones earlier in this chapter.

Fixed assets

These assets may be owned for a long time. They will retain at least some of their value over the long term and will be available to help generate revenue in the long term. The long term is usually taken to be a period longer than one year. It is not right to write them off to the profit and loss account immediately. Instead depreciation entries write them off over an appropriate period of time. Examples of fixed assets are freehold property, leasehold property, computers, fixtures and fittings, motor vehicles and plant and machinery.

The figure in the Smith and Jones balance sheet is £360,000. This will be the total amount paid for the freehold property, plant and machinery and the motor vehicles, less depreciation written off in the profit and loss account in the years since the assets were purchased.

In practice, it is rare for fixed assets to be worth exactly their written-down value in the books. The reasons are:

● The arbitrary nature of the depreciation rules
● Individual circumstances
● Inflation

Asset strippers specialize in finding companies where the fixed assets are worth more than the book value. They then purchase the company and unlock the value by selling some or all of the assets and realizing the profit.

Current assets

These are assets whose value is available to the business in the short term. This is either because they are part of the trading cycle (such as stock and trade debtors) or because they are short-term investments (such as a 90-day bank deposit account). The definition of short term is usually taken to be up to a year.

Debtors are usually current assets. The definition of a debtor is a person owing money to the business, such as a customer for goods sold. Examples of current assets are:

- Stock
- Trade debtors
- Bank accounts
- Short-term investments

The figure in the Smith and Jones balance sheet is £300,000.

Current liabilities

These are liabilities that the business could be called upon to discharge in the short term. Examples are trade creditors, bank overdrafts, taxation payable within a year and hire purchase payable within a year. The definition of a creditor is a person to whom the business owes money, such as a supplier.

The figure in the Smith and Jones balance sheet is £180,000.

Net current assets

This is also known as working capital and it is extremely significant. It is the difference between current assets and current liabilities, and it will be a negative figure if the liabilities are greater. It is very important, because net current assets are what are available to finance the day-to-day running of the business. If net current assets are insufficient for this purpose, the business may have to close or seek some other form of finance. It is possible for a business to be profitable but have to close due to a shortage of working capital.

The figure in the Smith and Jones balance sheet is £120,000.

Long-term liabilities

The Smith and Jones example does not include one, but these are liabilities which are payable after more than a year. An example could be a fixed-term bank loan. A business may be able to solve a shortage of working capital by obtaining a long-term loan in place of a bank overdraft.

Bank overdrafts are invariably legally repayable on demand. This means in theory, and very occasionally in practice, that the bank manager can demand repayment at 3 p.m. and, if payment has not been received, take action at 4 p.m. On the other hand, a long-term fixed loan is only repayable when stipulated by the agreement and according to the conditions of the agreement.

Let us consider a ten-year loan of £1,000,000, repayable by ten equal annual instalments of £100,000. The balance sheet would show £900,000 under the long-term liabilities and £100,000 under current liabilities. After a year, and one repayment, the balance sheet would show £800,000 under long-term liabilities and £100,000 under current liabilities. Hire purchase contract balances are split in the same way. The part repayable after a year is shown in long-term liabilities.

A business has an obvious incentive to make as many of its liabilities, as possible into long-term liabilities. This eases the pressure on working capital.

Capital and reserves

This is the 'net worth' of the business and is the bottom part of the balance sheet. The total figure for capital and reserves is the balance sheet total. The top part of the balance sheet is 'net assets' and comes to the same total. The figure for Smith and Jones is £480,000.

Capital and reserves together represent the investment of the owners in the business. In the case of a company, capital and reserves may be made up of some combination of:

- Share capital: there may be more than one class of share
- Revenue reserves: these are accumulated net profits from the past, after taxation, dividends and other distributions
- Capital reserves: these are reserves created in defined ways and only available for distribution in defined ways
- Profit and loss account: this is part of revenue reserves

Statement of financial position (or balance sheet) prepared in accordance with international financial standards (IFRS)

The following is the statement of financial position of Company A, whose income statement was shown yesterday. It is dated at the end of the trading period covered in that income statement and the profit is incorporated in it.

Company A

Statement of Financial Position as at . . . . .

	Notes	Current Date £000	Previous Date £000
Non-current assets			
Intangible assets – goodwill	8	162	162
Property, plant and equipment	9	83	52
Deferred tax asset	7	13	6
		258	220
Current assets			
Trade and other receivables	10	73	306
Cash and cash equivalents	11	492	344
		565	650
Total assets		823	870
Current liabilities			
Trade and other payables	12	(306)	(499)
Income tax payable		(50)	(24)
		(356)	(523)
Total liabilities		(356)	(523)
Net assets		467	347
Equity			
Equity share capital	16	250	250
Retained earnings		217	97
Total equity		467	347

As explained earlier in this chapter, the assets less the liabilities is £467,000 and this is the 'net worth' of the company. It represents the shareholders' investment in the company.

Note 8 relates to goodwill. This exists because in a previous year the company paid more than net book value for another company. This excess payment is left in its balance sheet. Note 8 explains why no impairment is necessary.

Note 9 gives details of the fixed assets, the depreciation charge in the year and net book value at the balance sheet date.

Note 11 reveals that the £492,000 is all represented by cash at the bank and cash in hand.

Note 12 gives the split of trade and other payables as:

	£000
Trade payables	156
Social security	20
Other payables	130
	306

Note 16 gives details of the authorized and issued share capital. There is only one class of share.

Balance sheet prepared in accordance with UK accounting standards

The following is the balance sheet of Company B, whose profit and loss account was shown yesterday. It is dated at the end of the trading period covered in that and the loss is incorporated in it.

Company B

Balance Sheet as at.....

	Note	Current Date £	Previous Date £
Fixed assets			
Goodwill	8	1,616,743	729,345
Tangible fixed assets	9	7,101,740	7,818,028
Investments	10	12,187,649	5,445,145
		20,906,132	13,992,518
Current assets			
Stocks	12	7,167,091	6,264,078
Debtors	13	6,163,713	4,601,141
Fixed-term deposits	15	2,191,436	12,381,235
Cash at bank and in hand		3,834,521	2,875,493
		19,356,761	26,121,947
Creditors, amounts falling due within one year	16	(3,129,758)	(2,114,299)
Net current assets		16,227,003	24,007,648
Total assets less current liabilities		37,133,135	38,000,166
Provisions for liabilities and charges	17	(303,320)	(665,366)
		36,829,815	37,334,800
Capital and reserves			
Called up share capital	18	100,000	100,000
Revaluation reserve	19	142,721	142,721
Profit and loss account	19	36,587,094	37,092,079
Equity shareholders' funds	19	36,829,815	37,334,800

I said yesterday that despite the loss the company was not threatened and had a secure balance sheet, and this can be readily seen. In fact it has more than six million pounds of cash and a 'net worth' of £36,829,815. Nevertheless, losses are, of course, bad news and there has been a deterioration over the year.

Company B's balance sheet has more notes than Company A's balance sheet. This is not because UK standards generate more notes than international standards. It is because the company is bigger and its structure is more complicated. As you would expect there is a mass of detail in the notes and they answer many of the questions that will occur to you.

Goodwill has increased due to acquisitions in the year but, unlike Company A, there has been amortization during the period. It is explained in note 8. You will probably notice the very big reduction in fixed-term deposits which is in current assets, and the big increase in investments which is in fixed assets. Details are contained in notes 15 and 10.

The directors' report states that business conditions were extremely challenging and that this was a main reason for the loss. In light of this it is interesting to see the increase in stocks and debtors, despite the reduction in turnover. Note 13 discloses that £954,261 of the increase in debtors was down to the increase in trade debtors. Customers were taking longer to pay.

Information that must be given

In the case of a company, the Companies Act and accounting standards require certain information to be given in the notes. If there is nothing to report under a particular heading, it is not necessary to have that heading in the notes. The following are many of the requirements.

Details of share capital and debentures

This includes separate details of authorized and issued share capital, details of any debentures and information about any redeemable preference shares. Since 1st October 2009, it has been possible to dispense with the concept of authorized share capital.

Details of tangible fixed assets and depreciation

Details of investments

Separate details for listed and unlisted investments must be given. Details of aggregate market value must be given if this differs from the balance sheet value.

Details of movements in reserves and provisions

Details of indebtedness

Convertible debt must be analysed between amounts falling due:

● In one year or less, or on demand
● Between one and two years
● Between two and five years
● In five years or more

In respect of debt that is due for repayment wholly or partly after five years, terms of interest and repayment must be stated. So too must details of any security given.

Details of any cumulative dividends in arrears

Details of any guarantees given

Details of capital commitments and other commitments at the balance sheet date

Details of contingent liabilities at the balance sheet date

A contingent liability is one that may never be realized. An example is a pending legal case which could result in the company having to pay damages. The company might win or the action might be withdrawn, but it could result in a future payment. To the extent that a reserve for this has not been created in the accounts, details should be given in a note. It is normal for directors to state their view of the likelihood of the contingency being realized.

Debtors

The analysis given in the note must separate sums falling due within one year from sums falling due after one year.

Post balance sheet events

For non-adjusting post balance sheet events and the reversal of a transaction which was entered into to alter the appearance of the balance sheet it is necessary to show:

- The nature of the event
- An estimate of the financial effect, or a statement that it is not practicable to make such an estimate
- An explanation of the taxation implications, where necessary for a proper understanding of the financial position

Summary

Today we have studied in some detail the balance sheet (or statement of financial position). We have:

- Seen what it is, its purpose and how it is fundamentally different from the profit and loss account.
- Seen how it is laid out to comply with both international and UK accounting standards.
- Studied the main balance sheet headings and the information that must be provided in accompanying notes.

The whole of tomorrow's work is going to be the study of a range of accounting ratios. It will be interesting and important.

SUNDAY

MONDAY

TUESDAY

WEDNESDAY

THURSDAY

FRIDAY

SATURDAY

Fact-check (answers at the back)

1. Which of the following statements is true about a balance sheet?
   a) It summarizes the assets and liabilities over a stated period ❑
   b) It summarizes the assets and liabilities at a stated date ❑
   c) It compares the profit with the assets ❑
   d) It is a more detailed version of the profit and loss account ❑

2. In which category in the balance sheet will plant and machinery be classed?
   a) Fixed assets ❑
   b) Current assets ❑
   c) Current liabilities ❑
   d) Capital and reserves ❑

3. During what period must liabilities be liable to be discharged in order to be classed as current liabilities?
   a) Up to three months ❑
   b) Up to six months ❑
   c) Up to one year ❑
   d) Up to two years ❑

4. Which of the following must be disclosed in notes to the accounts?
   a) Details of share capital and debentures ❑
   b) Details of any cumulative dividends in arrears ❑
   c) Details of contingent liabilities at the balance sheet date ❑
   d) All of the above ❑

5. What is represented by the total of the capital accounts?
   a) The total share capital ❑
   b) Share capital plus share premium ❑
   c) Revenue reserves ❑
   d) The net worth of the business at book value ❑

6. Does a registered company have a legal existence and personality separate from the shareholders who own it?
   a) Sometimes ❑
   b) Yes ❑
   c) No ❑
   d) Only if it is insolvent ❑

7. Does the business of a sole trader have a legal existence and personality separate from the person who owns it?
   a) Sometimes ❑
   b) Yes ❑
   c) No ❑
   d) Only if it is insolvent ❑

8. This chapter gives the Smith and Jones partnership balance sheet at 30th April. How much is owing to the partnership?
   a) £130,000 ❑
   b) £120,000 ❑
   c) £300,000 ❑
   d) £480,000 ❑

9. This chapter gives the Smith and Jones partnership balance sheet at 30th April. If the partnership was terminated, assets realized £50,000 less than book value and the winding up expenses were £10,000, how much money would Smith get?
a) £240,000 ☐
b) £230,000 ☐
c) £220,000 ☐
d) £210,000 ☐

10. A company took a bank loan of £6,000,000 two years ago. It is repayable over five years in 60 equal monthly instalments. How will the remaining balance be shown in the balance sheet?
a) £3,600,000 in current liabilities ☐
b) £3,600,000 in long-term liabilities ☐
c) £1,200,000 in current liabilities and £2,400,000 in long-term liabilities ☐
d) £1,800,000 in current liabilities and £1,800,000 in long-term liabilities ☐

THURSDAY

Using ratios to interpret accounts

This is a useful and interesting chapter. In fact you may well find it the most interesting chapter in the whole book. We looked at some profit and loss ratios on Tuesday and today's chapter consists of commonly used balance sheet and investment ratios. Some of them are illustrated by figures from the accounts of Company A and Company B which appeared in previous chapters. You may need to look back at them.

When you have finished this chapter it would be a good idea to get a set of accounts and work out the ratios for yourself. If you do this, I hope that you do not get any nasty surprises. It is easily possible to get hold of the accounts of companies registered in the UK. Monday's chapter gives details of how it can be done.

The ratios covered today are:

- Return on capital employed
- Gearing
- Stock turn
- Liquidity
- Number of days, credit given
- Number of days, credit taken
- Dividend cover
- Dividend yield
- Earnings per share
- Price earnings ratio

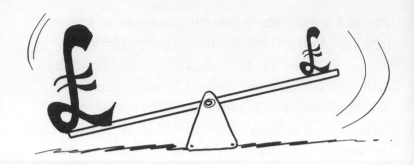

Return on capital employed

This is often abbreviated to ROCE and sometimes given the alternative name of 'return on investment' or ROI. It is profit expressed as a percentage of the net value of the money invested in the business. Many people believe that it is the most important of the accounting ratios.

Capital employed is the balance sheet total, which in the case of a company is share capital plus reserves. This is 'shareholders' funds', which is the same as assets less liabilities. Sometimes profit before tax is used and sometimes profit after tax is used. Exceptional items may be included or excluded and so may interest. Profit after interest and after tax is the most commonly used figure.

Normally, the profit for the year is compared with capital employed, as shown in the balance sheet at the end of the year. However, it is better (though in practice perhaps unnecessary) to use the average capital employed throughout the year. To obtain this you will need at least the opening and closing balance sheets.

Using the figure for profit after tax, Company A's return on investment is 25.7 per cent. The calculation is:

$$\frac{120}{467} \times 100 = 25.7 \text{ per cent.}$$

Return on investment is obviously influenced by the profit, but it should not be forgotten that it is also affected by the capital employed. Suppose that Company A had a target of getting its return up to 30.0 per cent. It might do this by raising the profit after tax to £140,000. The return on capital employed would then be:

$$\frac{140}{467} \times 100 = 30.0 \text{ per cent.}$$

It could also do it by reducing the capital employed to £400,000, in which case the return on capital employed would be:

$$\frac{120}{400} \times 100 = 30.0 \text{ per cent.}$$

There are a number of ways that capital employed might be reduced. Company A has money in the bank so the payment of a dividend might be considered.

Gearing

This ratio compares the finance provided by banks and other lenders with the capital provided by the owners. It is much used by banks who might not like to see a ratio of 1 to 1 (or some other such proportion) exceeded. It is sometimes expressed as a proportion, as in 1 to 1, and sometimes as a percentage. The following is an example of the calculation.

	£000
Loans	4,300
Shareholders' funds	5,968
Gearing	0.7 to 1

A company is said to be lowly geared when borrowing is low in relation to shareholders' funds, and this indicates a secure, safe position. An adventurous, though perhaps foolish, person might say that it indicates a boring position. A consequence is that a change in profits, up or down, will have less effect on return on capital employed than if the company had been highly geared. On the other hand, a company is highly geared when borrowing is high in relation to shareholders' funds, and this indicates a position that is less secure and less safe. A consequence is that a change in profits, up or down, will have a big effect on return on capital employed. The following figures illustrate this:

	Company X	Company Y
Loans (in £000s)	40,000	160,000
Shareholders' funds (in £000s)	160,000	40,000
Gearing	1 to 4	4 to 1
Profit after tax (in £000s)	16,000	4,000
Return on capital employed	10.0%	10.0%

Both companies are achieving a return on capital of 10 per cent but Company B is much more highly geared. Now look at what happens if both companies increase their profits by £3 million:

	Company X	Company Y
Loans (in £000s)	40,000	160,000
Shareholders' funds (in £000s)	160,000	40,000
Gearing	1 to 4	4 to 1
Profit after tax (in £000s)	19,000	7,000
Return on capital employed	11.9%	17.5%

Your reaction may be that it is better to be highly geared. This may well be true if the business is secure and highly profitable, but look what happens if profits drop by £3 million:

	Company X	Company Y
Loans (in £000s)	40,000	160,000
Shareholders' funds (in £000s)	160,000	40,000
Gearing	1 to 4	4 to 1
Profit after tax (in £000s)	13,000	1,000
Return on capital employed	8.1%	2.5%

There are, of course, many ways of looking at the figures and it is up to you to draw sensible conclusions in individual circumstances. It is certainly true that many spectacularly successful businesses have been highly geared, but it is also true that many spectacular collapses have occurred in similar circumstances.

Stock turn

This is the number of times that total stock is used (turned over) in the course of a year. The calculation for Company B is as follows:

	£000
Cost of sales for year	12,076
Stock at balance sheet date	7,167
Stock turn	1.7 times

You probably think that this is poor and I would agree, though we should remember that individual circumstances not known to us could be relevant. Company B is a manufacturing company so materials, direct labour, etc. will be in the cost of sales.

Cost of sales should be obtainable from the profit and loss account, and stock should be obtainable from the balance sheet. However, a word of caution is necessary. The balance sheet gives the stock figure at a single date and that date may not be typical of the profit and loss period, especially if the company is expanding or contracting, or if the business is seasonal. A more reliable figure for stock turn might be obtained if the average of several stock figures during the period is used, though in practice this might be difficult to obtain. Fortunately, published accounts must give comparable figures for the previous period and balance sheet date.

It is usually reasonable to conclude that the higher the stock turn the better, and that a high stock turn is an indication that a business is being efficiently run. Some years ago certain Japanese companies became famous for their 'just in time' ordering systems, and a few even managed to maintain stock levels measured in production hours, rather than days, weeks or months. The rest of the world has been catching up and British supermarkets are examples of businesses that are very efficient in this respect, though some suppliers have been known to complain that the success has been obtained at their expense.

Despite all the advantages of a high stock turn the theory should not be tested to destruction. It is not efficient to run out of stock, have to suspend production or leave customers staring at empty shelves. It may be wise to keep higher stocks of key components or the most popular items for sale. It may also be wise to keep higher stocks if the sources of supply are insecure or not responsive to an increase in demand. A company vulnerable to industrial disputes at its suppliers is an example.

Liquidity

Companies are not forced into involuntary liquidation because they are not making profits, although this is, of course, extremely unhelpful. It is, perhaps surprisingly, not uncommon for companies to go into liquidation that are trading profitably at the time. This is particularly true of companies that have expanded rapidly. The immediate cause of business failure is usually that they run out of liquid resources and cannot pay their debts as they become due. A balance sheet will reveal vital information about working capital and liquid resources, and it is possible that impending problems may be predicted.

A balance sheet should (and a published balance sheet must) separate assets capable of being turned into cash quickly from assets held for the long term. The former are called current assets. Similarly, a balance sheet should separate liabilities payable in the short term (current liabilities) from those payable in the long term. The dividing point is usually one year.

The difference between current assets and current liabilities is the working capital. This is sometimes called net current assets, or net current liabilities if the liabilities are greater. The position for Company B is as follows:

	£000
Current assets	19,356
Less current liabilities	3,129
	16,227

This is a very safe position.

Another frequently used ratio is the so-called quick ratio or acid test. This is more demanding than the working capital calculation because, of the current assets, only debtors, investments, bank and cash are used, and the total of these is compared with the total of current liabilities. Only the most liquid of the current assets are brought into the calculation. Stock is excluded because it almost always takes longer to turn into cash than debtors. If stock is excluded, the position for Company B is as follows:

	£000
Applicable current assets	12,190
Less total current liabilities	3,129
	9,061

Number of days' credit given

This is the average period of credit taken by customers in paying their bills. The calculation for Company B is as follows.

	£000
Turnover	22,680
Trade debtors at year end	4,761
Number of days credit	76.6 days

Trade debtors at year end is obtained from a note. The calculation is:

$$\frac{4,761 \times 365}{22,680} = 76.6 \text{ days}$$

Two problems should be kept in mind:

1 The turnover for the year is compared with trade debtors at a fixed date. If the figure for trade debtors is not typical of the year as a whole, the result may be misleading.
2 Turnover will very probably exclude VAT, whereas the trade debtors figure will, if it is applicable, include it.

At the time of writing, the standard VAT rate in the UK is 20 per cent. If, in the above example, all the trade debtors included 20 per cent VAT, the real figure for the purposes of the calculation would be 3,967. The revised calculation would be:

$$\frac{3,967 \times 365}{22,680} = 63.8 \text{ days}$$

Number of days' credit taken

This is, of course, the mirror image of the number of days' credit given. However, you will only be able to do the calculation if you have extra information beyond that disclosed in the published accounts. This is because the figure for purchases will not be given in the profit and loss account. The figure for total costs will include such things as salaries and depreciation. The following example (not taken from Company B) assumes that it has been possible to ascertain the figure for annual purchases:

	£000
Annual purchases	64,717
Trade creditors	9,245
Number of days' credit	52.1 days

The calculation is:

$$\frac{9{,}245 \times 365}{64{,}717} = 52.1 \text{ days}$$

Dividend cover

This compares the annual dividend to equity shareholders with profit after tax. It is important because it helps indicate whether or not a company has a problem paying its dividend, and whether or not the dividend may be increased, maintained or reduced in the future. The following illustrates the calculation.

	£000
Profit attributable to shareholders	3,015
Dividends on equity shares	920
Dividend cover	3.3 times

Dividend yield

This is the dividend per share expressed as a percentage of the current share price. The following illustrates the calculation.

Shares in issue	10,000,000
Dividends paid	£934,000
Dividend per share	9.34 pence
Current share price	£1.21
Dividend yield is	$\frac{9.34}{121} = 7.7$ per cent

Earnings per share

This is the net profit after tax divided by the number of issued shares. The following illustrates the calculation.

Net profit after tax	£3,015,000
Number of shares issued	10,000,000
Earnings per share	30.15 pence

Price earnings ratio

This is one of the most helpful of the investment ratios and it can be used to compare different companies in different sectors. It is often utilized to make a judgement about whether a particular company's shares are relatively cheap or relatively expensive. The higher the number, the more expensive the shares. It is often useful to do the calculation based on anticipated future earnings rather than declared historic earnings. Of course you cannot always, or indeed ever, be certain what future earnings will be.

The calculation is quoted price per share divided by earnings per share. The following illustrates the calculation.

Current share price	£1.64
Earnings per share	30.15 pence
Price earnings ratio	$\frac{164}{30.15} = 5.4$

This seems a low ratio so perhaps the shares are worth buying, but, on the other hand, perhaps there are good reasons for the unfavourable rating. The profit and loss account and balance sheet reflect past performance. Perhaps the up-to-date figures are very different.

Summary

We have spent the whole of today studying ten commonly used balance sheet and investment ratios. This is using the accounts creatively in order to really understand the significance of the figures. The ratios are useful and important in themselves and they enable the accounts of different businesses to be compared. Please do not forget the traps and warnings detailed on Sunday. The ratios have to be interpreted and put into context.

There are three further aspects of the reports and accounts package. The reports are a matter of words and we will end the week by considering them. Tomorrow it is cash flow and group accounts.

SUNDAY

MONDAY

TUESDAY

WEDNESDAY

THURSDAY

FRIDAY

SATURDAY

Fact-check (answers at the back)

1. Capital employed is 10 million pounds, fixed assets are 4 million pounds, current liabilities are 7 million pounds and profit after tax is £560,000. What is the return on capital employed?
   a) 40.0 per cent ❑
   b) 5.6 per cent ❑
   c) 10.0 per cent ❑
   d) Nil ❑

2. Which of the following statements applies when a company is said to be highly geared?
   a) Borrowing is high in relation to shareholders' funds ❑
   b) Borrowing is low in relation to shareholders' funds ❑
   c) Borrowing is approximately the same as shareholders' funds ❑
   d) There is no borrowing ❑

3. Cost of sales for the year is £6,629,431. Stock at the year end is £912,844. What is the stock turn?
   a) 5.3 times ❑
   b) 5.9 times ❑
   c) 6.7 times ❑
   d) 7.3 times ❑

4. What does net current assets comprise?
   a) Total assets less total liabilities ❑
   b) Total assets less current liabilities ❑
   c) Current assets less current liabilities ❑
   d) Total assets less shareholders' funds ❑

5. Turnover is £16,256,311 and trade debtors at the year end are £1,345,621. What is the number of days' credit granted?
   a) 28.6 days ❑
   b) 30.2 days ❑
   c) 37.9 days ❑
   d) 43.4 days ❑

6. Purchases in the year are £3,671,222 and trade creditors at the year end are £863,116. What is the number of days' credit taken?
   a) 39.0 days ❑
   b) 61.3 days ❑
   c) 85.8 days ❑
   d) 96.4 days ❑

7. Profit after tax attributable to shareholders is £17,341,269. Dividends on equity shares are £4,250,000. What is the dividend cover?
   a) 3.1 ❑
   b) 4.1 ❑
   c) 5.1 ❑
   d) Zero ❑

8. Shares in issue are 5,000,000. Dividends paid in the year were £1,000,000. Current share price is £2.33. What is the dividend yield?
   a) 11.6 per cent ❑
   b) 8.9 per cent ❑
   c) 5.0 per cent ❑
   d) 17.2 per cent ❑

9. Net profit after tax is £2,623,111. Number of shares issued is 5,000,000. What is the earnings per share?
a) 26.2 pence ☐
b) 50.0 pence ☐
c) 19.0 pence ☐
d) 52.5 pence ☐

10. Net profit after tax is £2,623,111. Number of shares issued is 5,000,000. Current share price is £6.84. What is the price earnings ratio?
a) 11.0 ☐
b) 12.0 ☐
c) 13.0 ☐
d) 14.0 ☐

FRIDAY

Cash flow statement and group accounts

Today we examine the two things identified in the heading to this chapter. I suspect that you will find the cash flow statement more difficult than group accounts.

'Cash is king' is a well-known saying often attributed to Jim Slater, the famous financier. He became, in his words, a minus millionaire, but later recovered much of his fortune. Today we will see why cash is so important and we will examine the many differences between cash and profit.

The cash flow statement explains the movement of cash into and out of the business during the period covered by the accounts. It identifies the difference in cash between the two balance sheet dates and it reconciles this difference with the profit and loss in the period. We will have a close look at two examples.

The final part of our work is the subject of group accounts. We will see why they are necessary, in what circumstances they must be prepared and their key features.

The topics covered today comprise:

- The differences between cash and profit
- The importance of cash and working capital
- The concept of the cash flow statement
- Cash flow statement for company using UK accounting standards
- Statement of cash flows for company using international accounting standards
- Group accounts

The differences between cash and profit

Cash is most definitely not the same as profit. Most people know this, so my apologies if I am telling you what you already know and what seems obvious, but a surprising number of people are confused on the point. You may well have heard comments such as 'Don't be silly. We can't have run out of money – we are making a profit'. Cash and profit (apart from dividends, etc.) may be the same in the very long term or when a business is wound up, but they will almost certainly be different (perhaps very different) at any given time. The following are some of the reasons:

Dividends

Dividends are a distribution of profit, not a charge against profit (in the way that salaries and other expenses are a charge against profit).

Capital expenditure and depreciation

Payment for capital expenditure is usually immediate or nearly so, but the effect on profit is spread over a number of years. Consider a motor car that is purchased for £30,000 on the first day of the accounting year. Unless it is being bought on hire purchase, £30,000 cash will go out of the business at or near the beginning of the year. On the other hand it will probably be depreciated over four years, so £7,500 will be charged to the profit and loss account in the first year. In that year the effect on cash will be £22,500 worse than the effect on profit. In the following year there will be no effect on cash but a further £7,500 depreciation charge to the profit and loss account.

Investments

The purchase of investments will take cash out of the business but will have no effect on the profit and loss account. The effect will be the opposite when the investments are sold.

Loans

A loan to the business puts cash into the business but has no effect on profit, though of course interest will probably have to be paid. A loan made by the business will have the opposite effect.

The purchase of stock for resale

This normally has to be paid for shortly after it is purchased. The goods purchased only affect the profit and loss account when they are sold, which is usually later.

Bad debt reserve and other reserves

The creation of a bad debt reserve or other reserve reduces the profit but has no effect on the cash. Time will eventually show whether the reserve was correct, too high or too low, and the difference will then be unwound.

Tax

In the UK, corporation tax (for a company) and income tax (for a sole trader or partnership) are normally paid to HMRC after the trading period to which they relate.

Timing differences relating to sales and purchases

Sales are usually credited to the profit and loss account when goods are delivered or services performed. Payment is usually received from customers later. Purchases are usually debited to the profit and loss account as they are made. Suppliers are usually paid later.

The importance of cash and working capital

It is tempting, but of course wrong, to say that cash is the notes and coins found in the petty cash box. This is part of cash, but only a very small part. Cash is the total of all the bank balances plus any notes and coins. The bank balances almost always make up virtually all the cash total. Bank overdrafts must be deducted. It is possible, and indeed very common, for total cash to be a minus figure. Cash for Company B at the balance sheet date is the apparently large sum of £6,025,957 (fixed-term deposits of £2,191,436 plus cash at the bank and in hand of £3,834,521). These figures can be seen in the balance sheet that was reproduced in Wednesday's chapter.

Working capital is net current assets, which is the difference between current assets and current liabilities. Working capital is usually a positive figure and the bigger the figure the bigger the margin of safety. If working capital is a negative figure, it is a very worrying sign of possible trouble and at the very least a reason for asking searching questions. Working capital for Company B is the seemingly very large sum of £16,277,003.

It is possible, and indeed it is not uncommon, for a business to fail even though it is making profits at the time of its failure. This is because it does not have enough cash to pay its suppliers as the debts fall due for payment. Profits are obviously very desirable and very important, and in the long term they provide the means to pay the suppliers, but in the short term it is necessary to have cash.

It is possible, and quite common, for a very profitable, rapidly expanding business to run out of cash. This is because a rapidly expanding business usually has an increasing need for working capital. Cash goes out of the business before a greater amount of cash comes into the business. It may be necessary to take on more staff and pay them and it may be necessary to take larger premises. It may be necessary to buy more stock to meet the greater volume of orders.

This does not, of course, mean that a business should not be profitable and rapidly expanding. It means that the owners should ensure that it does have sufficient cash and working capital. Perhaps more share capital should be injected into the company. Perhaps steps should be taken to convert a short-term bank overdraft into a long-term bank loan. Perhaps the payment of dividends should be stopped for a while. There are many possibilities.

Working capital and cash are both very important. The control of working capital is a step towards the control of cash. If working capital is adequate, it is likely that cash will be adequate or at least that cash will become adequate in the near future.

It is not possible to give the 'right' figures or proportions for cash or working capital, though it is possible to state categorically that they should be sufficient. This is because businesses vary and circumstances vary. If there is a sure source of further capital or resources if needed, it may be possible to operate with smaller working capital. It is also very helpful if the suppliers value the business and are willing to be supportive.

It is possible to have too much cash and too much working capital. This is wasteful because money is tied up in working capital that could profitably be invested elsewhere. Alternatively, the surplus money could be paid out to the owners of the business. Working capital should be sufficient but not excessive.

The concept of the cash flow statement

This can be stated very simply, although it often gets complicated in practice. The difference between the cash totals in two balance sheets is identified. The two balance sheets are the ones at the beginning and end of the profit and loss period. The various factors affecting the difference are identified and listed, so that the reasons for the change in the cash totals are explained. There are usually notes to support the figures in the statement.

If UK accounting standards are used, it is called the cash flow statement. If international accounting standards are used, it is called the statement of cash flows. They do the same job but the rules about layout are different.

The information disclosed is interesting and valuable. One reason for this is that, short of fraud, it is virtually impossible to cheat. It is sometimes said that profit is partly a matter of opinion. This is inevitable for a number of reasons. For example, it is necessary to take a view on the value of stock and this in turn has an effect on profit. Cash, on the other hand, is very much a matter of fact. It is there or it is not there.

Cash flow statement for company using UK accounting standards

Following is the cash flow statement of Company B, together with notes 23, 24 and 26. All this is taken from the company's financial statements package. The profit and loss account is shown in Tuesday's chapter and the balance sheet is shown in Wednesday's chapter. We will then examine the layout and what the figures reveal.

	Note	Current Year £	Previous Year £
Net cash (outflow)/inflow from operating activities	23	(817,026)	663,643
Returns on investments and servicing of finance	24	164,819	156,890
Taxation	24	(109,795)	397,568
Capital expenditure and financial investment	24	(6,864,216)	(2,424,999)
Acquisitions and disposals	24	(1,288,095)	–
Management of liquid resources	24	10,189,799	(5,253,148)
Net cash outflow before financing		1,275,486	(6,460,046)
Equity dividends paid	19	(300,000)	(300,000)
Increase/(decrease) in cash in the year	26	975,486	(6,760,046)

Note 23: Reconciliation of operating loss to operating cash flows

	Current Year £	Previous Year £
Operating loss	(826,930)	(830,433)
Depreciation	930,177	846,034
Amortization	267,017	–
Impairment of investment	–	75,000
Profit on disposal of tangible fixed assets	(54,241)	–
(Increase)/decrease in stocks	(250,043)	257,917
(Increase)/decrease in debtors	(805,506)	1,356,658
Decrease in creditors	(77,500)	(1,041,533)
Net cash (outflow)/inflow from operating activities	(817,026)	663,643

Note 24: Analysis of cash flows

	Current Year £	Previous Year £
Returns on investments and servicing of finance		
Interest received	164,819	156,890
Taxation		
UK corporation tax refunded	(109,795)	(397,568)
Capital expenditure and financial investment		
Purchase of tangible fixed assets	(468,977)	(215,526)
Sale of tangible fixed assets	347,265	9,585
Purchase of fixed asset investments	(6,750,000)	(3,778,310)
Sale of fixed asset investments	7,496	1,559,252
Net cash outflow from capital expenditure and financial investment	(6,864,216)	(2,424,999)
Acquisitions and disposals		
Net cash acquired with subsidiary	68,655	–
Cost of purchase of subsidiary	(1,356,750)	–
	(1,288,095)	–
Management of liquid resources		
Decrease/(increase) in fixed-term deposit	10,189,799	(5,253,148)

Note 26: Reconciliation of net cash flow to movement in net funds

	Current Year £	Previous Year £
Increase/(decrease) in cash	975,486	(6,760,046)
Cash flow from changes in debt	(10,189,799)	5,253,148
Net debt acquired with subsidiary	(2,093)	–
Change in net funds raising from cash flows	(9,216,406)	(1,506,898)
Net funds at beginning of year	15,240,270	16,747,168
Net funds at end of year	6,023,864	15,240,270

The operating loss, shown in the profit and loss account, was £826,930, but despite this the cash flow statement shows an increase in cash during the year of £975,486. This rather conveniently illustrates the point that cash and profit are not the same thing. It is one of the jobs of the cash flow statement and relevant notes to identify the factors that caused the difference.

The increase of cash of £975,486 is calculated as follows:

	£
Cash at bank and in hand – current year	3,834,521
Cash at bank and in hand – previous year	2,875,493
	959,028
Add previous year overdraft eliminated in current year	16,458
	975,486

The first two figures are taken directly from the balance sheet. The separate overdraft of £16,458 is disclosed in a note that is not reproduced in this chapter.

The statement shows that a dividend of £300,000 was paid during the year and this, of course, is a cash distribution and does not affect the profit. After adding this back the figure to be explained is £1,275,486.

The operating loss in the profit and loss account is £826,930. Note 23 lists the various factors that moved this figure to a net cash outflow of £817,026, which is the first figure in the cash flow statement. Hopefully everything in note 23 will be understood. To take just one item, the figure of £930,177 for depreciation is favourable for cash. This is because it is a non-cash charge to the profit and loss account and must therefore be added back.

Explanations for the remaining items in the cash flow statement are given in note 24. Once again, hopefully it will all be understood. To explain just one figure, cash outflow of £1,288,095 related to the purchase of a subsidiary company.

It all comes together, though I realize that understanding it all will be challenging. Note 26 shows how the company gets from £975,486 to net funds at the end of the year. Net funds is not quite the same thing as the definition of cash. The figure of £6,023,864 is made up as follows:

	£
Fixed-term deposits	2,191,436
Cash at bank and in hand	3,834,521
	6,025,957
Less net debt acquired with subsidiary	2,093
	£6,023,864

The first two figures come from the balance sheet and the last figure comes from note 26.

Statement of cash flows for company using international accounting standards

The concept is of course the same and the details have a lot of similarities, but there are some differences. The cash flow statement is divided into three sections, but companies may decide which section is most appropriate for a particular heading in light of their individual circumstances. The three headings are:

- Operating activities
- Investing activities
- Financing activities

The following is the statement of cash flows for Company A and, you may be relieved to know, it is an extremely simple example. They can be much longer and much more complicated. The income statement for Company A was included in Tuesday's chapter and its statement of financial position was included in Wednesday's chapter.

	Note	Current Year £000	Previous Year £000
Operating activities			
Profit for the year		120	46
Adjustments			
Tax on continuing operations		46	22
Depreciation and impairment of property, plant and equipment		36	35
Decrease/(increase) in trade and other receivables		233	(183)
(Decrease)/increase in trade and other payables		(194)	129
Cash generated from operations		241	49
Income taxes paid		(26)	(9)
Net cash flow from operating activities		215	40
Investing activities			
Payments to acquire property, plant and equipment		(67)	(20)
Net cash flows from investing activities		(67)	(20)
Increase in cash and cash equivalents		148	20
Cash and cash equivalents at the beginning of the year	11	344	324
Cash and cash equivalents at the year end	11	492	344

The profit for the year of £120,000 is after tax and is taken from the income statement. The figure of £492,000 for cash and cash equivalents is taken from the statement of financial position. Only two of the three required headings are used. This is because there is nothing to report under the heading of 'financing activities'.

It is possible that you might be puzzled by the cash inflow of £233,000 caused by the decrease in trade and other receivables. The calculation is:

	£
Trade and other receivables at beginning of period	306,000
Less trade and other receivables at end of period	73,000
	233,000

Less is owing to the company, which means that payments have come in, which in turn means that there has been a cash inflow. Like so many things in accounts the figures need interpreting. Perhaps customers have paid more quickly and the credit controllers have done a good job, but there could be other reasons. Perhaps there was very little invoicing at the end part of the year and consequently there was less money to collect at the balance sheet date.

Group accounts

Why are group accounts necessary? Please consider the following group structure and the following circumstances.

Devonshire Widgets Ltd owns 100 per cent of the shares in the three other companies. Devonshire Widgets Ltd pays £50,000 for a consignment of widgets and sells them to Plymouth Widgets Ltd for £100,000. This company sells them to Torquay Widgets Ltd for £200,000 and they are in stock at the balance sheet date. The accounts of Devonshire Widgets Ltd show a profit of £50,000 and the accounts of Plymouth Widgets Ltd show a profit of £100,000. The accounts of Torquay Widgets Ltd show stock of £200,000 and no profit or loss effect. Furthermore and as a separate matter, the four balance sheets (all with the same date) disclose the following.

- Devonshire Widgets Ltd owes £600,000 to Plymouth Widgets Ltd
- Plymouth Widgets Ltd owes £600,000 to Torquay Widgets Ltd
- Torquay Widgets Ltd owes £600,000 to Exeter Widgets Ltd
- Exeter Widgets Ltd owes £600,000 to Devonshire Widgets Ltd

Without group accounts the accounts of each company would be misleading. The consequences of group accounts mean that the effect of inter-group trading is eliminated. Revenue is only recognized when sales outside the group are made. In the example, if and when Torquay Widgets Ltd sells the widgets outside the group for £330,000 it will recognize a profit of £130,000. The group profit and loss account will then show sales of £330,000, cost of sales of £50,000 and a profit contribution of £280,000. Until that happy day there will be no effect on the group profit and loss account, and the group balance sheet will include the widgets with a stock value of £50,000. Furthermore, the group balance sheet will net off all the intercompany debts of £600,000 and it will show nothing payable or receivable in respect of them.

Each company in a group is required to prepare and file at Companies House its own individual accounts, even though they contribute to group accounts.

A parent company/subsidiary company relationship exists when the parent company is in one of the following positions:

- Holds a majority of the voting rights
- Is a member and has the right to appoint or remove directors holding a majority of the voting rights at meetings of the board
- Has the right to exercise a dominant influence over the other company:
  a) by virtue of provisions contained in the undertaking's articles; or
  b) by virtue of a control contract
- Is a member and controls alone, pursuant to an agreement with other shareholders or members, a majority of the voting rights in the undertaking
- Has a participating interest and:
  a) it actually exercises a dominant influence over it; or
  b) it and the subsidiary undertaking are managed on a unified basis

A participating interest is an interest held on a *long-term basis* for the purpose of securing a contribution to its activities by the exercise of control or influence. A holding of 20 per cent of the shares is a participating interest, unless it is shown not to be so.

Group accounts need not be presented where one of the following applies:

- The company is not listed on the stock exchange of an EU member state and is more than 50 per cent owned by a parent undertaking established in an EU member state, and is included in its group accounts drawn up in accordance with the seventh directive
- No member of the group is a public company and the group qualifies as a small or medium-sized group
- The subsidiary companies are not material
- The rights of the parent company are subject to long-term restrictions
- Inclusion would cause disproportionate expense or delay
- The parent company's interest is held with a view to resale
- The activities are so different that inclusion would be incompatible with a true and fair view

Summary

We have covered a lot of ground today and some of it has been quite challenging. Well done if you have grasped all the points. We have:

- Noted that profit is most definitely not the same thing as cash, and we have seen some of the reasons why this is not the case.
- Seen why cash and working capital is so important.
- Discovered the purpose of a cash flow statement (statement of cash flows if international accounting standards are used).
- Studied in detail real-life examples of a cash flow statement and a statement of cash flows.
- Seen why group accounts may be necessary, some key principles of group accounts and in what circumstances group accounts are required.

This book is entitled *Understanding and Interpreting Accounts In A Week* but your accounts come with reports. Indeed the package is usually called the 'Reports and Accounts'. Tomorrow is our final day and we will move on to the reports.

SUNDAY
MONDAY
TUESDAY
WEDNESDAY
THURSDAY
FRIDAY
SATURDAY

Fact-check

1. It is called the cash flow statement if UK accounting standards are used. What is it called if international accounting standards are used?
   a) Cash movement statement ❏
   b) Cash statement ❏
   c) Cash variation statement ❏
   d) Statement of cash flows ❏

2. What are dividends?
   a) A distribution of profit ❏
   b) A charge against profit ❏
   c) Net profit after tax ❏
   d) A bookkeeping entry that does not affect cash ❏

3. Ignoring interest, what does a loan to the business affect?
   a) Profit ❏
   b) Cash ❏
   c) Both profit and cash ❏
   d) Neither profit nor cash ❏

4. Cash in the petty cash box is £200 and the bank overdraft is £100,000. What is the cash figure for most purposes?
   a) £200 positive ❏
   b) £100,000 negative ❏
   c) £99,800 negative ❏
   d) £100,200 negative ❏

5. What does a cash flow statement link?
   a) The cash position in two balance sheets ❏
   b) Two profit and loss accounts ❏
   c) The profit and loss account and the balance sheet ❏
   d) Net assets in two balance sheets ❏

6. Trade and other receivables in the previous balance sheet was £80,000. Trade and other receivables in the current balance sheet is £230,000. What is the effect on the cash flow statement?
   a) £150,000 outflow ❏
   b) £150,000 inflow ❏
   c) £230,000 outflow ❏
   d) £230,000 inflow ❏

7. A company sells goods to its subsidiary company for £60,000. The subsidiary company sells half the goods outside the group for £50,000 and has the remainder in stock at the balance sheet date. What amount must be shown in sales in the group profit and loss account?
   a) £60,000 ❏
   b) £50,000 ❏
   c) £30,000 ❏
   d) £100,000 ❏

8. The directors believe that the accounts of a small subsidiary company are not material. Must group accounts be prepared?
   a) Yes, always ❏
   b) Usually ❏
   c) Not usually ❏
   d) No ❏

9. What does depreciation affect?
   a) Both cash and profit ❏
   b) Neither cash nor profit ❏
   c) Profit ❏
   d) Cash ❏

10. Is it difficult to manipulate
    the figures in the cash flow
    statement?
a) Yes – short of fraud it is
   virtually impossible   ❑
b) It is fairly difficult   ❑
c) It is fairly easy   ❑
d) It is very easy   ❑

SATURDAY

The reports

During the first six days of the week we have tried to understand and interpret accounts, which are very much a matter of figures. Today we round off the week by looking at the reports, which are largely a matter of words. Directors of registered companies have a legal obligation to accompany the accounts with certain reports. These give factual information beyond what is in the accounts and help the reader understand and interpret the figures and the company's strategy and position.

This chapter relates to UK companies. It may be different in other countries and it is different for other types of organization. There is a lot to get through and it might be hard going, but it will hopefully be worth the effort.

The topics covered today comprise:

- Directors' report
- Directors' report in a publicly traded company
- Directors' report in a small company
- Business review
- Remuneration report
- Other reports and information
- Audit report

Directors' report

The Companies Act and regulations made under its authority require directors to provide a directors' report with the statutory accounts. Its contents are prescribed by law, although if there is nothing to report under a particular heading it may be omitted. The required disclosures are as follows:

Directors' names

The report must give the names of all persons who were directors for any part of the year, with dates of becoming a director and ceasing to be a director if applicable.

Principal activities

This shows the principal activities of the company in the course of the year. There may be more than one.

Proposed dividend

The amount (if any) of a dividend that the directors propose should be paid.

Disclosure to auditors

Unless the company is claiming exemption from audit, the directors' report must state that:

- So far as the directors are aware, there is no relevant audit information of which the company's auditor is unaware
- All directors have taken all the steps that they ought to have taken as directors in order to make themselves aware of any relevant audit information and to establish that the company's auditor is aware of that information

It is a criminal offence to make this statement without the belief that it is true, and it is binding on the directors individually as well as collectively.

Any difference in market value of land

If, in the opinion of the directors, the market value of land owned by the company differs from its book value, the report must disclose this fact. This is only if the directors are of the opinion that the members' (this usually means the shareholders,) attention should be drawn to it.

Political donations

Details must be given if political donations exceed £2,000 in total.

Charitable donations

Details must be given if charitable donations exceed £2,000 in total. Wholly owned subsidiary companies incorporated in the UK are excluded from this requirement and so is money given for charitable purposes outside the UK. The reason for this exclusion escapes me. £2,001 donated to a British charity must be disclosed but not 10 million pounds given to an Australian one.

Financial instruments

Details of the use of financial instruments must be given if this is material for an assessment of the company's financial position. This sounds rather boring but it can be vastly important. Significant companies have collapsed due to problems with financial instruments.

Post balance sheet events

Details must be given of any important events that have taken place since the date of the balance sheet. This could be very significant indeed. Public companies have six months to publish their accounts and private companies have nine months, but even if the directors do it quickly the accounts are out of date by the time they are read.

An indication of likely future development of the business

This could be very significant.

An indication of the activities in research and development

Many companies will have nothing to report but, for example, a major drugs company will probably have a lot to report and it could be of critical importance.

An indication of the existence of branches outside the United Kingdom

This is only necessary for limited companies, but all but about 4,000 companies are limited companies.

Details concerning any acquisitions of its own shares by the company or its nominees

This is rare but it is legal in some circumstances.

Disabled employees

The following is only required if the average weekly number of employees is greater than 250, excluding employees who work wholly or mainly outside the UK:

There must be a statement describing the policy which the company has applied during the year for:

- Giving full and fair consideration to applications for employment from disabled persons
- Continuing the employment of, and training of, employees who have become disabled whilst employed by the company
- The training, career development and promotion of disabled persons employed by the company

I ask your indulgence for a personal question and a personal point of view. Have you ever seen a directors' report that does not describe the company's policy in generous and compassionate terms? No – neither have I, even though some companies do not in practice live up to what they say are their policies. I rather doubt the value of the requirement, but perhaps I am rather cynical.

Information for employees

The following is only required if the average weekly number of employees is greater than 250, excluding employees who work wholly or mainly outside the UK.

There must be a statement describing the action taken during the year to introduce, maintain or develop arrangements intended to:

- Provide employees systematically with information on matters of concern to them as employees
- Consult employees or their representatives on a regular basis so that their views can be taken into account in making decisions likely to affect their interests
- Encourage the involvement of employees in the company's performance through an employee share scheme or other means
- Achieve a common awareness on the part of all employees of the financial and economic factors affecting the performance of the company

In practice a rather bland statement is often given. My personal views are the same as set out in the part about disabled employees. I have never seen a directors' report that says company policy is to only give employees the minimum possible information.

Payment of suppliers

The following must be given for public companies and for large private companies that are subsidiaries of public companies:

- A statement of policy on the payment of suppliers
- If the company subscribes to a code on payment practices, such as the CBI code, this must be stated, and it must also be stated how details of the code may be obtained
- A statement of the average number of days, credit outstanding at the balance sheet date

It is not unknown for companies to 'window dress' the average number of days, credit outstanding by making extensive payments just before the balance sheet date. Sadly, it is also by no means unknown for companies to actually pay suppliers in a way completely different from the stated policy. Some powerful and well-known companies do it. You can probably name some of them.

Directors' report in a publicly traded company

A publicly traded company is one which at the end of the relevant period has securities traded on a regulated market. This does not include AIM. Such companies must provide the information previously listed in this chapter. The lengthy list of additional information includes:

- The structure of the company's capital
- In the case of each person with a significant direct or indirect holding of securities in the company, such details as are known to the company of:

  a) The identity of the person
  b) The size of the holding
  c) The nature of the holding

Directors' report in a small company

The definition of a small company was given in Monday's chapter. If you have a good memory, you will recall that it is that in two successive years, and counted on a group basis, the company satisfied two out of three conditions. One of these was that turnover did not exceed £6,500,000.

The directors' report with the accounts sent to the members (this usually means the shareholders) must disclose:

- The names of the persons who were directors at any time during the year
- The principal activities of the company during the year
- Political donations exceeding £2,000 in aggregate
- Charitable donations exceeding £2,000 in aggregate
- If the average number of employees exceeds 250, a statement describing the company's policy towards the employment, training and career development of disabled persons
- Disclosures concerning acquisition by the company of its own shares during the period

This relates to the accounts sent to the members and nothing need be included if there is nothing to report under the heading. No directors' report is required for the abbreviated accounts that small companies may send to Companies House.

Business review

Unless the company is a small company, the directors' report must include or be accompanied by a business review. Its purpose is to inform the members (this usually means the shareholders) and help them assess how the directors have performed their duty to promote the success of the company. The business review must contain:

- A fair review of the company's business
- A description of the principal risks and uncertainties facing the company
- A balanced and comprehensive analysis of the development and performance of the company's business during the financial year
- A balanced and comprehensive analysis of the position of the company's business at the end of the year, consistent with the size and complexity of the business

This is for all companies that are required to have a business review. More information is required if the company is a quoted company. This includes (but is not limited to):

- The main trends and factors likely to affect the future development, performance and position of the company's business
- Information about environmental matters (including the impact of the company's business on the environment, the company's employees and social and community issues)
- To the extent necessary for an understanding of the development, performance or position of the company's business an analysis using key performance indicators

The business review can be fascinating and valuable. This is more likely when directors approach it in the right spirit and aim to increase the reader's understanding. The opposite approach is a box-ticking exercise intended merely to comply with their legal obligations.

Remuneration report

The remuneration report is only a requirement for quoted companies. The remuneration in question is that of directors and there is a legal requirement that a mass of information be given. The reports are frequently 15 or more pages long. If you read everything thoroughly, it will probably take quite a while and it will probably be very interesting, especially as much of the disclosure is for each director by name.

Some of the information is subject to audit and some is not. The part that is not subject to audit includes the following:

- Information regarding the members of and advisers to the remuneration committee
- A statement of the company's policy on directors' remuneration for the following financial year including details on performance conditions
- A performance graph that sets out the total shareholder return on the class of equity share capital that caused the company to fall within the definition of 'quoted company'
- Information regarding directors' contracts of service

The part that is subject to audit includes considerable detail concerning salaries and fees, bonuses, expenses, compensation for loss of office, non-cash benefits, share options, long-term incentive schemes, pensions, excess retirement benefits of directors and past directors, compensation paid to past directors and sums paid to third parties in respect of a director's services.

There must be a separate vote of the shareholders on the remuneration report at the meeting at which the accounts are laid, which is usually the annual general meeting. This vote is advisory only and not binding on the directors. However, in practice directors and others take it seriously. A vote to reject the remuneration report is a serious matter and can lead to changes in policy, better reporting and explanation, changes to the remuneration committee and even resignations of directors.

Until relatively recently a vote to reject the remuneration report was almost unknown, but although still rare such votes have become more common. So too have votes where there have been a significant number of abstentions. Many people believe that directors' pay is out of control. The Government has plans to move towards making the vote binding rather than advisory, but at the time of writing this has not yet happened.

Other reports and information

The law prescribes information that must be included in the reports and most companies comply with the law, provide the information and leave it at that. However, some companies choose to go beyond this minimum, even though it is quite an extensive minimum. They may, for example, provide a chairman's report or extend the directors' report beyond the statutory requirement. It is not unknown for the directors (and the chairman in particular) to give their views on such matters as bureaucracy, interest rates and the government of the day.

Listed companies are required by the listing rules to give more information than other companies and may choose to give more still. For example, the latest reports and accounts of Marks and Spencer Group plc consists of 112 pages and it is more for some listed companies. It contains, among other things, a chairman's statement, a chief executive's review, a section on 'performance and marketplace', and a section on governance. Some of the material in these sections provides information required by the directors' report and the business review, and these documents refer the reader to the appropriate section.

Audit report

Monday's chapter gives details of when an audit report is required. The auditor gives an opinion but does not certify the accuracy of the figures, a point which auditors are keen to stress but which is often misunderstood.

The first duty of the auditor is to give an opinion as to whether the accounts give a 'true and fair view' and whether or not the information in the directors' report is consistent with the accounts. They must also give an opinion as to whether the part of the remuneration report that is subject to audit has been properly prepared. There is more, but that will do for the purposes of this chapter.

The audit report almost always gives a favourable opinion on these matters. This is partly because of the integrity and professionalism of most directors, but also because of their fear of the consequences of a qualified audit report. If the auditor threatens to qualify the report, most directors will, with greater or lesser grace, agree to the necessary changes.

Some audit qualifications may be technical and not too worrying, but you should certainly take a qualified audit report seriously. Normally a quick glance for assurance is all that is necessary.

Summary

Today we have looked at the reports which must accompany the financial statements of a company registered in the UK. If you are a person who thrives on mastering a lot of information, you will have coped admirably and probably enjoyed it. If you are not a detail person, it will have been more difficult, but well done for persevering. On our final day we have:

● Studied a list of the detailed information that must, by law, be included in the directors' report. This has included the special provisions for publicly traded companies and small companies.

● Looked at the business review, which gives extra information and helps us understand the company's position, key indicators and strategy.

● Seen the remuneration report which, for understandable reasons, is often the part of the accounts package that gets most media attention and sometimes provokes indignation. If you are a highly paid director, you might think that this is unfair and disproportionate. If the company is a bank and you are one of its shareholders or customers, you might (or might not) think that this is very understandable.

● Examined the contents of the audit report.

SUNDAY
MONDAY
TUESDAY
WEDNESDAY
THURSDAY
FRIDAY
SATURDAY

Fact-check (answers at the back)

1. What is the basis for the information that must be provided in the directors' report of a registered UK company?
   a) The law ❏
   b) Accounting standards ❏
   c) The wishes of the directors ❏
   d) Common sense ❏

2. Ruth Cohen became a director on 8th February and resigned with effect from 12th June in the same year. What (if any) details must be included in the directors' report for the year to 31st December?
   a) Nothing must be included ❏
   b) The name and the starting and finishing dates must be given ❏
   c) Just the name must be given ❏
   d) The name and the starting date must be given ❏

3. The directors' report must include a statement that relevant information has been disclosed to the auditor. On which directors is this binding?
   a) The directors as a group ❏
   b) Just on directors who have held office for the whole year ❏
   c) The directors as a group and each director individually ❏
   d) Only on directors who wish to be associated with the statement ❏

4. A company has given £6,100 to the Labour party. Must this be disclosed in the directors' report?
   a) No ❏
   b) Only if it is a listed company ❏
   c) Only if the amount is significant in relation to the company's turnover ❏
   d) Yes ❏

5. A UK company has given £7,103 to a US charity that helps homeless people in the state of Arizona. Must this be disclosed in the directors' report?
   a) Yes ❏
   b) Only if the company has business in the United States ❏
   c) Only if the company does not have business in the United States ❏
   d) No ❏

6. The directors' report must contain a statement about the company's policy on the payment of suppliers. To which companies does this apply?
   a) All companies ❏
   b) Public companies and large private companies that are subsidiaries of public companies ❏
   c) All companies except small companies ❏
   d) Public companies ❏

7. A company has a turnover of £8,246,137 and it has employed an average of 253 people. Does it qualify as a small company for the purposes of the directors' report?
a) Yes ☐
b) Only if its balance sheet total is less than £3,260,000 ☐
c) No ☐
d) Yes – unless it is a public company ☐

8. Must a large private company include in its business review information about environmental matters?
a) Yes ☐
b) Only if the company produces hazardous waste ☐
c) Only if a trade union requests it to do so ☐
d) No ☐

9. Must a remuneration report include a statement of the company's policy on directors' remuneration for the following financial year?
a) Yes – but this part of the remuneration report is not subject to audit ☐
b) Yes – and this part of the directors' remuneration report is subject to audit ☐
c) Only if the policy has changed ☐
d) No ☐

10. For whom is the audit report primarily intended?
a) The directors ☐
b) The members (this usually means the shareholders) ☐
c) The government ☐
d) The European Union ☐

NB The information needed to answer question 10 is not given in the chapter so if you have got 69 questions out of 69 correct, you should look on it as a tiebreaker. Congratulations if you get it right.

Surviving in tough times

Times are tough. They have been tough for most of us for some time, and they will probably be tough for some time to come. Let us hope that this prediction is wrong, but we would be well-advised to remember the adage 'Hope for the best and prepare for the worst'. Understanding and interpreting accounts can be of crucial importance in surviving tough times. It is a four-stage process. You need to have the information, you need to understand the information, you need to interpret the information and, most importantly, you need to act on the information. It is rather like a sinking ship. It is useful to know that the ship is sinking and helpful to know why it is sinking, but then you need to stop it sinking or, if all else fails, launch the lifeboats. Here are ten crucial tips to help you survive.

1 Never neglect cash

Cash is the lifeblood of the business. Profit is good. In fact profit is very good, but it does not pay the salaries next Tuesday. You need cash to do that. Monitor the cash position and cash projection frequently, daily if necessary. Give cash very high priority and do what is necessary to make sure that the business has enough of it.

2 Never neglect working capital

Working capital is the same as net current assets. This in turn is the difference between current assets and current liabilities. Current assets are ones that can be realized in the short term and current liabilities are ones that are payable in the short term. The bigger the difference, the bigger the margin of safety, and it can be a negative figure, which should be very worrying indeed. Keep a close eye on working capital, act early and do what you can to keep it healthy. Much can be done: not overstocking is just one example.

3 Control the receivables

Receivables are sometimes called trade debtors and they are money owing to the business by customers. You should always take credit control seriously, but especially when times are tough. You should agree the period of credit with your customers and then hold them to it. Some will forget to pay on time and many will deliberately pay late. Do not let them get away with it. They are cheating you.

4 Try and see that there are no nasty surprises

This may be easier said than done, but try hard to make sure that you are not taken unaware by bad news. Understanding and interpreting the accounts of your business is a big step towards achieving this. Try to get the accounts early then examine and interpret them quickly. Do not put them to one side.

5 Try and have friends

You may be familiar with the saying 'Be nice to people on the way up, you might meet them on the way down'. Being nice to people and having friends has to be a good idea anyway, but there are very practical advantages when times are tough. This is the time when you might need to call in favours. If you have in the past helped the person that you are asking and if there is mutual liking and respect, you are more likely to get a favourable response.

6 Get the gearing right

Gearing is the relationship between the finance provided by banks and other lenders with the capital provided by the owners. So, for example, 2 million pounds of loans and 1 million pounds of share capital is a ratio of 2 to 1. The higher the ratio, the higher the risk, and of course also the higher the possible reward for success. Shareholders cannot demand their money back, so plan for the owners to have the necessary investment. This was explained on Thursday.

7 Do not put too many eggs in one basket

You may be vulnerable if you only have a small number of customers, and desperately vulnerable if you only have one or two. If one of these goes bust, the resulting bad debt and loss of future business could cripple you. Even if this does not happen you may be in a weak position to resist slow payment or unreasonable terms of business. It may be easier said than done and a small number of customers is almost inevitable in some businesses, but be aware of the risks.

8 Be realistic

Ostriches are popularly supposed to deal with danger by putting their heads in the sand so that they cannot be seen, but ostriches are silly birds and this tactic will not help them. It will not help you either. Danger will not go away if you pretend that it is not there. Find the facts and the risks, and intelligent use of the accounts is an important part of doing this, then plan to do what is necessary. Optimism is fine, but it must be tempered by realism.

9 Make comparisons

'We are not alone' – the quote is from the much-loved film E.T. and it is true in business too. Accounts can tell you a lot about your business and they can tell you a lot about your competitors' businesses. They are not likely to provide their accounts for you, but if your competitor is a company you can get hold of a copy. Put it next to yours and compare the figures and the ratios. Where they are better try to work out why and how you can close the gap.

10 Do not take too much out

The point of most businesses is to provide money for their owners. If the business is a company, the money is usually taken out as dividends, though if it is owner-managed it might be by means of salary, bonuses, fringe benefits or possibly some other way. If the business is not a company, it will be salary, bonus, drawings, etc. I am sorry to say this, but tough times may mean that less money should be taken out and more left in to pay the bills. Fairly obviously, smaller dividends, or no dividends at all, leave more cash in the business and healthier working capital.

Answers

Sunday: 1c; 2d; 3c; 4b; 5b; 6c; 7d; 8c; 9a; 10b.

Monday: 1b; 2d; 3a; 4d; 5a; 6a; 7c; 8a; 9b; 10b.

Tuesday: 1c; 2a; 3b; 4d; 5b; 6d; 7a; 8c; 9c; 10b.

Wednesday: 1b; 2a; 3c; 4d; 5d; 6b; 7c; 8a; 9d; 10c.

Thursday: 1b; 2a; 3d; 4c; 5b; 6c; 7b; 8a; 9d; 10c.

Friday: 1d; 2a; 3b; 4c; 5a; 6a; 7b; 8d; 9c; 10a.

Saturday: 1a; 2b; 3c; 4d; 5a; 6b; 7c; 8d; 9a; 10b.

The Teach Yourself series has been trusted around the world for over 60 years. This series of 'In A Week' business books is designed to help people at all levels and around the world to further their careers. Learn in a week, what the experts learn in a lifetime.

Roger Mason is a Chartered Certified Accountant with many years' practical experience as a Finance Director at a number of global companies. He now lectures on financial and business topics. In addition, he has edited a financial publication and written many books.